RUNNING YOUR

ANDREW FRAZIER, MBA, CFA, SBPRO

SMALL BUSINESS LIKE A PRO UNIVERSITY PRESS
NEW JERSEY

Of all the people I have collaborated with; Andrew Frazier is the real deal. He fundamentally understands the challenges small businesses face and can quickly develop real world solutions that drive impressive results, which I have seen firsthand. Plus, he can help you quickly assess your business fundamentals with his Value Builder assessment tool, making it easier for him to help you take your business forward.

Gene Bohensky

President, The Alternative Board Northern New Jersey
Certified Business Coach and Value Builder, Archer Strategies

Andrew and "Small Business Like A Pro" are much needed voices and champions of the country's largest employers – small business collectively. The book is a practical must-read and belongs in the library of anyone who owns a small business and especially those who aspire to the enterprise ranks and "to be able to have their business function independently of the owner." The book is also a valuable resource for coaches and consultants who want an easy to understand reference they can use to help increase the operational competence of their small business clients.

David Greene

President
Urbanomics Consulting Group

Within the pages of "Running Your Small Business Like A Pro", Andrew Frazier provides readers with his candid perspectives on overcoming key challenges that small business owners face. The book's examples clearly demonstrate how Mr. Frazier applies his comprehensive business background to help small business owners, many of which have invested all to realize their dreams, transform their ideas and plans into sustainable enterprises.

John E. Harmon, Sr. IOM

CEO, African American Chamber of Commerce of New Jersey
Former Chairman, National Black Chamber of Commerce

Andrew's book is a handy guide for small business owners to know what to check, why and how they need to check it, and most importantly it provides a prescribed course of action for you to follow. You'll get lots of reality checking and no holds barred truth telling. The powerful case studies clearly demonstrate the path he follows to guide companies from challenge to opportunity and serve as social proof for the credibility of his remedies. This line from the book's title page says it all: "The More You Know, The Faster You Grow."

Arthur Jones
Principal Consultant
The Art of Standing Out, LLC

"The Small Business Pro methodologies outlined in the book have helped many Rising Tide Capital entrepreneurs not only survive but thrive."

Alfa Demmellash
CEO
Rising Tide Capital

I read your book Thursday night as I could not put it down ... such a simple take on such a complex topic and laid out steps that we all can take to move our own businesses forward. I wish I had this 'map' when I started my own businesses!

- *My favorite Section - What You Don't Know WILL Hurt You!*
- *Without Sales & marketing, You Have No Business."...Yes!*
- *Key Learnings - lead the book, these take-aways are critical. I like that they were captured and re-captured throughout.*

Dr. John Kennedy
Chief Executive Officer
New Jersey Manufacturing Extension Program, Inc.

Andrew Frazier has a commitment and passion to helping small businesses gain access to the tools and techniques necessary to enable them to successfully grow and thrive in today's dynamic environment. His book outlines the techniques any business in any industry sector can deploy to achieve long term sustainability. In addition, Andrew's support of the urban small business community makes him a true asset in the New Jersey entrepreneurial ecosystem.

Judith Sheft

Executive Director

New Jersey Commission on Science, Innovation and Technology

"This is a true common sense guide. It tells you how to run your enterprise like a business, not a pastime or hobby. For those who need direction on the important basics for success, this is the book for you."

John J. Webb

CEO and Managing Partner

Quantum Reach

The key strategies to achieve success in small businesses are often different from those of larger businesses. The primary difference is the amount of time you must spend working IN the business versus ON the business. I found this challenge and others outlined well in, "Running Your Small Business Like a Pro", by Andrew Frazier. He recommends some key techniques, learned by both of us the hard way, that every small business owner can and must deploy to achieve long-term sustainability and growth.

Martin Zwilling

Founder and CEO

Startup Professionals

This book is available at special discounts for bulk purchases, sales promotions, premiums, fundraising, or educational use.

For details, e-mail: info@SmallBusinessLikeAPro.com

Small Business Pro University Press
email: info@SmallBusinessLikeAPro.com
Website: www.SmallBusinessLikeAPro.com

Copyright © 2018, 2020 Andrew Frazier Jr,

Cover Design and Layout: Andrew Frazier Jr.
Diagram Illustrator: Andrew Frazier Jr.
Editors: Barry Cohen and Joycelyn Frazier
Photographer: Tamara Fleming

Library of Congress Control Number: xxxxxxxxxx

ISBN 978-1-970129-02-1

Printed in the United States of America

Second Edition: June 2021

Dedication

To my Family

To my wonderful wife Janae, my daughter Joycelyn who is beginning her college experience at Kingston University in London, and my son Andrew III (Tre) who is on track to earn the rank of Eagle Scout this year, thank you for supporting me through all the ups and downs associated with my being an entrepreneur.

To my late Uncle Dennis "Buddy" Strong Jr., CIMC

I appreciate you taking the time to patiently impart the wisdom of a world class management consultant. Thank you for trekking from Barbados to New York in the middle of winter to be the featured guest speaker at my POWER BREAKFAST event. I will continue to pass on the knowledge you shared with me to others who can truly benefit from it.

To Small Business Owners and Entrepreneurs

I appreciate you making things happen every day in pursuit of the American dream. There are those who watch what happened, there are also those who make things happen, and then there are those who wonder what happened. Thank you for taking the road less traveled and going out onto the field of play. It is my pleasure and honor to share what I have learned to help you become even more successful in your business endeavors.

Acknowledgements

It has been 40+ years since embarking on a small business journey with my brother Evan, owning a paper route for the "Pittsburgh Press". My path has been long and windy yielding many outstanding learning opportunities. Graduating from MIT, serving in the Navy, and working for a large private company strengthened my analysis, operations, and leadership skills. Pursuing an MBA at NYU, working at major corporations, earning a Charter Financial Analyst (CFA) designation, and nonprofit leadership roles developed my finance, administrative, and management expertise. Finally, coming full circle to my entrepreneurial roots through serving as a coach, consultant, and trainer of entrepreneurs and small business owners for the past 10 years. I have had a great ride, met thousands of great people along the way, and can't wait to see what lies ahead.

I am grateful to God for guiding me through this process of writing *Running Your Small Business Like A Pro*. He blessed me with patience and His wisdom throughout the multi-year journey to complete this book.

I could not have finished without so much support along the way. Thanks to my family, friends, colleagues, business partners, clients, and network of mentors for all your encouragement and support throughout the process.

Arthur Jones was instrumental in my development of the Small Business Like A Pro concept during our many really-long phone conversations about small business. He helped me discover the story behind my leadership journey and understand how it translates into who I am and what I do. Art would read through book drafts providing brutally honest feedback about where it was lacking. He constantly challenged me to communicate the story behind the message, rather than just facts. His efforts helped make the book a much easier and more enjoyable read than it otherwise would have been.

This book would have never been completed if it wasn't for my book coach / consultant, Barry Cohen, Owner of AdLab Creative. I'll always appreciate his patience and encouragement throughout the journey. Barry would call exactly on time for our sessions and always ask "What can I do to help you get this completed?" He went above and beyond eliminating obstacles and helping me overcome the negative impact of choosing to drop typing class in 12th grade. His expertise and insights proved extremely valuable throughout the entire writing process.

Alfa Demmellash is truly a pioneer in transforming lives and communities through entrepreneurship. A very special thanks for her generous contribution in writing the Foreword. I am deeply honored and humbled to have her support and involvement in this way.

My daughter Joycelyn, a second year student at Kington University studying Creative Writing and English, made a valuable contribution in helping to edit this book. She made sure that I stayed on point and communicated the concepts in a way that everyone could understand them. I especially appreciate her taking time on her birthday to do a final review of the book before I sent it to print. Joycelyn plans to have a career in publishing, starting out as an editor. Good thing I caught her on the way up while I can still afford her services!

Victor Nichols, CEO of DMC Publishing, for reviewing my manuscript during his vacation. It was very encouraging to hear that he found the content engaging and felt it would be very helpful for small business owners. I also appreciated him cautioning me not to try and make it perfect because then I would never finish. As an added bonus his wife, an editor, went through the draft and marked it up for me.

I greatly appreciate Rising Tide Capital, the Small Business Development Center (SBDC), and the New Jersey Manufacturing Experience Program (NJMEP) for the opportunity to work with their entrepreneur and small business owner clients. These experiences allowed me to gain useful knowledge in the process of helping them. These interactions were instrumental in building my expertise and recognizing the patterns that led to the development of the SBPro Critical Path and SBPro Methodology.

Special thanks to all of my clients, especially those who allowed me to use their experiences as an example for others. I have enjoyed working with you and look forward to participating in your continuing success.

Last but not least, I want to thank my younger brother, Evan Frazier, for completing his book, *Most Likely to Succeed: The Frazier Formula for Success,* 10 years ago. It is a great resource that positively impacted the lives of many, which is also my goal. I used his book as a template and source of inspiration. Despite our competitive nature, he was extremely supportive and encouraging throughout the entire process.

Thank you for purchasing this book, which is just the beginning of our journey. I invite any feedback, comments, and ideas that you may have to make it more valuable for others. Please share any needs, wants, and desires you have for small business resources, connections, and information that could be helpful. We look forward to developing a comprehensive platform to serve the needs of entrepreneurs in the region, across the country, and throughout the world.

Table of Contents

Foreword

I learned so many lessons from my mother who fled her native Ethiopia in 1982 after the Red Terror, living first in a refugee camp and later in Boston. She would waitress in the mornings and sew gowns in the evenings - a small business she'd founded to earn extra income to bring me to live with her in the United States. After surviving a brutal dictatorship in Ethiopia, a decade long separation from my mom, and a kidnapping, I came to the U.S. without knowing a lick of English and attended Harvard five years later. Without my mother's perseverance and her small business, who knows where I would be or what I would be doing.

These early life experiences combined with the need to learn English upon arrival in the US and the challenges of integrating into a new culture, have given me a deep belief that anything is possible. They have also given me an appreciation for the importance of entrepreneurship in hardworking underserved communities. That understanding drove me to found Rising Tide Capital, a nonprofit organization in New Jersey. Our mission is to transform lives and communities through entrepreneurship. Our vision is to be a catalyst for economic and social empowerment.

Rising Tide Capital provides business development services designed to transform lives by helping individuals start and grow successful businesses; building communities through collaborations with other nonprofits, higher education institutions, corporations, and public agencies; and creating a scalable program model with measurable impact which can be replicated in communities of need across the United States.

We exist to help entrepreneurs like you start or grow your business by providing the highest quality business management, planning, and support services. Andrew Frazier is one of our top business coaches, working with more than 100 of our entrepreneurs and business owners over the past 5 years. He has helped many of them grow revenues and increase profitability using the SBPro Methodology of "Running Your Business Like A Pro." He has also led our initial Loan Readiness Coaching Program and has helped Rising Tide Capital business owners obtain more than $500,000 in financing. In addition, he has been a popular instructor in our flagship 12-week Community Business Academy program.

The Rising Tide Capital journey began in Jersey City, New Jersey during 2004. Since then we have been recognized by President Obama for social innovation, celebrated the 2,500th graduate of our Community Business Academy and launched innovative new programs to better serve the needs of our entrepreneurs. Initially, we expanded into Newark, New Jersey and have since expanded into four cities outside of New Jersey. The first of many national replication initiatives of the Rising Tide Capital model launched in Chicago. We remain dedicated to our vision and will continue to innovate in service to our mission.

Without dedicated coaches and instructors like Andrew, who develop and inspire our entrepreneurs, we cannot achieve our mission. He has contributed greatly to our organization and the success of our entrepreneurs. I am excited that *Running Your Small Business Like A Pro* is available as a great resource for our coaches, instructors, and entrepreneurs. Especially since the SBPro methodologies outlined in the book have helped many Rising Tide Capital entrepreneurs not only survive but thrive.

Use the lessons from *Running Your Small Business Like A Pro* to prepare for your upcoming business opportunities as well as your inevitable challenges. If you consistently apply the SBPro methodology, you too will find that nothing is impossible. Keep your eyes open, your thoughts positive, and commit to learn continuously. Your imagination is your best friend. The future promises constant change and your ability to imagine, to adapt, and to be patient with yourself as you manage the creative process will open countless opportunities for success. Whatever you do, don't let fear of failure or success get in the way of actualizing your dreams and goals. You, too, can Run Your Business Like A Pro!

Sincerely,

Alfa Demmellash
CEO
Rising Tide Capital
www.RisingTideCapital.org

Preface

Running Your Business Like A Pro shares valuable insights gained from coaching and consulting with over 500 small business owners, as well as my business leadership roles and entrepreneurial endeavors. It is a compilation of key learning and important perspectives gained from my diverse experiences with many different organizations.

As a coach to small business owners, I noticed several common patterns and themes:

1) Many key strategies to achieve success in small business are very different from those that make larger businesses successful. Small businesses must be much more creative and flexible to compete effectively.

2) There is a specific path that small businesses must follow to grow beyond self-employment. Unfortunately, most small businesses never reach that stage.

3) Most small business owners don't really understand their business model and the impact of the relationships among different parts of their business. As a result, their business runs them, as opposed to them running it.

4) Very few business consultants and coaches take a holistic approach to helping small business owners become more successful. Typically, they are experts in one business function (i.e. sales, online marketing, technology, operations, accounting, etc.) but are not very knowledgeable in others.

5) There is so much that small business owners need to know, and it is impossible to know everything. However, they must continually be learning, as well as surrounding themselves with those who have complementary skill sets.

In addition to working one-on-one with small business owners, I teach accounting, entrepreneurship, and finance courses. I have also been producing a series of POWER BREAKFAST events for entrepreneurs, business owners, and organizational leaders with more than 1,000 attendees over the past 7 years. We supercharge their day by providing a forum for attendees to learn business best practices, enjoy great networking with other business owners, and gain useful knowledge that they can put to work with their organizations immediately. The featured guest speaker at each event is a world class small business thought leader. We also provide post-event workshops and panels facilitated by experts within the local business ecosystem.

Running Your Small Business Like A Pro is the next step in the evolution on my path to help entrepreneurs and small business owners successfully navigate the numerous challenges they face. It is a 3-pronged strategy specifically designed as a guide for those who seek the knowledge and expertise that they need to thrive. It incorporates Brain Trust Initiatives (events and activities), Advisory Services (coaching, consulting, and training), and a Knowledge Center (resources, content, and certification). By using the Small Business Pro (SBP) methodology outlined in this book, you can learn what must be done to develop and grow your small business successfully.

To illustrate, I was once told a story about a leading business person who was asked about the secret of her success during an interview. She said that, "The secret to my success is making good business decisions." The interviewer asked, "That's great and all, but how did you learn how to make those good business decisions?" She responded, "By making bad business decisions and learning from them."

The key to becoming a successful entrepreneur and business owner is learning how to make the best decisions possible. There are two primary ways to gain the knowledge that you need to succeed in business. Either by losing money or through planning and preparation. Which one do you prefer?

By reading *Running Your Small Business Like A Pro*, you will learn how to plan more effectively and better understand the key drivers of your business. This book will also give you an opportunity to learn lessons from some of the bad decisions I and other entrepreneurs have made in the past. Although you will still make mistakes because we all do, you will be better prepared to build an even more successful business much faster and easier than otherwise possible.

I'm glad that you chose this book as a resource and I appreciate the opportunity to participate in your entrepreneurial journey. I look forward to guiding you along the path and it is my honor to provide you with some of the encouragement, education, and expertise needed to achieve your business goals. Let's get started.

Sincerely.

Andrew Frazier, MBA, CFA
Business Pro @ Small Business Like A Pro

Introduction

The Problem

Companies are facing greater challenges than ever before because of competitive pressures to continually innovate and adapt to new technologies in today's global business environment. It is tough out there for all companies, but especially difficult for small businesses because of their limited business expertise, fewer resources, and less access to capital. Unfortunately, small business owners often don't seek help until they are forced to do so - when they hit the proverbial wall. It can seem almost impossible for small businesses owned by minorities, women, and veterans in urban areas to effectively compete since they tend to have even less expertise, resources, and access to capital. However, they can learn to thrive by taking advantage of their size, flexibility, and creativity to deliver a unique value proposition for customers in the right target market.

Running Your Business Like A Pro is a wake-up call for small businesses owners. It is a call to action, along with a proven formula for adapting to thrive in any business environment. It provides key information, competent guidance, and valuable tools to assist you throughout your journey. This book outlines the critical path that small business owners need to follow. The book focuses on providing support in three key areas where they need the most help:

1.   Business Knowledge – small business owners understand their product/service but not the business model nor some of the best practices needed to succeed in business.

2.   Relationships – small business owners tend to work in isolation rather than developing a broad network and a team to support their growth.

3.   Resources – small business owners are not aware of the numerous resources available to them and seek assistance much later than they should.

Small businesses have consistently played a major role in economic growth because they create so many jobs - many more than large businesses. In 2014, according to the US Small Business Administration (SBA), small businesses added 1.4 million new jobs, 39% of which were from very small businesses (with fewer than 50 employees). That said, let's look at the mortality rate of small businesses. About two-thirds of businesses survive 2 years in business, while only half of all businesses survive 5 years, and less than one-third survive 10 years. According to a U.S. Bank study, a whopping 82% of businesses that fail, do so because of cash flow problems. The top 3 challenges of running a business, according to the small businesses surveyed by the National Small Business Association (NSBA) report are: economic uncertainty, the cost of health insurance benefits, and a decline in customer spending.

Obtaining enough financing is a problem for some as 27% of businesses surveyed by the NSBA claimed that they couldn't receive the funding they needed. For them, the most frequent primary impact that a lack of funding had was preventing them from growing their business, especially for women and minorities. Pepperdine University has done similar surveys, directly reaching out to small businesses about access to capital with similar results.

The current economy known as the "Gig Economy" provides both positive and negative dynamics for small business owners. A study by Intuit predicted that by 2020, 40% of American workers would be independent contractors. The forces behind the rise in short-term jobs in this digital age include globalization, corporate downsizing, an increasingly mobile workforce, aging out of workers with legacy skills that have not updated themselves, and the ability to do work from almost anywhere. That means that you can hire freelancers from around the world for temporary jobs and projects, allowing you to cost effectively employ the best individuals from a larger pool of candidates. However, this also means that there will be more people becoming freelancers and starting small businesses resulting in additional competitors.

The Solution

This book covers material that will provide you with many insights about running your business like a pro. The chapters in Section I – "What you don't know will hurt you!" outlines key learnings from my experience coaching and working with entrepreneurs and small business owners. Each one focuses on addressing a major challenge for small business owners, along with solutions by providing important insights, actual examples, and useful activities. Chapters in Section II – "This is how you do it!" outline my SBPro assessment and methodology for "Running Your Small Business Like A Pro." They provide a step-by-step process for guiding your journey toward growth and achieving the goals identified for your life and business. Also, you can practice what you are learning and enhance your business knowledge with the *Running Your Small Business Like A Pro Workbook*.

Section I – What You Don't Know WILL Hurt You!

Chapter 1 – How Did I Get Here?

Rationale

There are three drivers of why people go into business 1) for personal reasons, 2) professional aim, and 3) financial motivation, or a combination of the three. Personal reasons include freedom, flexibility, or stability. Is that why you went into business? Professional aims often include finding that dream job, self-actualization, or just making a difference. Is Financial motivation of making money, becoming that why you became an entrepreneur? wealthy, or successful. Of course, it's business, so hopefully a financial motivation is part of your rationale. Regardless of whether your reasons were implicit or explicit, you had certain expectations about the future benefits of becoming a business owner.

While this is the case, most entrepreneurs and small business owners have not achieved their original vision for becoming an entrepreneur. Many of them are also not sure if or how they can achieve it. As a result, they get stuck in a rut and are not able to move their organization to the next level. Have you ever been there?

If so, this book is definitely for you!

SBPro® Business Rationale

Copyright © 2018 Andrew Frazier Jr. All Rights Reserved

Purpose

It's important to know and be clear about the purpose of your business. Your purpose will drive your business planning and strategies. It also impacts how you should measure success. I look at businesses in terms of having one of four distinct categories:

1. **Hobby** - an activity that you engage in "for sport or recreation, not to make a profit." Even if you earn occasional income from doing such an activity, the primary purpose is something other than making a profit.

2. **Nonprofit** - organized for purposes of accomplishing a mission, rather than generating profit, and in which the organization's income is distributed for the greater good.

3. **Self-Employment** - individual who earns income through conducting profitable operations from a trade or business that he or she operates directly.

4. **Enterprise** - a business-oriented organization formed specifically so founders can show initiative and take risk to pursue expanding entrepreneurial endeavors for a profit.

For example, our family business started out as a hobby business. Initially my grandfather opened a dry-cleaning business in Pittsburgh, while also working two full-time jobs. Although he did work there and make money, it was referred to as his pet business because it was a way for him to get out of the house and spend time with friends. Over time, it grew and became more of self-employment once he retired from his previous jobs. When my grandfather's health was failing several years later, my uncle purchased the business and sought to grow it as an enterprise. He ended up purchasing another dry-cleaning business, opened several storefronts, and secured contracts from various companies. He still owns it and is in the process of transitioning the business to his son.

Also, for some businesses, the mission is focused on the wants, needs, and desires of the entrepreneur as opposed to their customers and making money. Sometimes these businesses can be difficult to sustain, depending on whether they can find a target market willing or able to purchase their products or services. Many times, they would fare better as a nonprofit and should probably be one. I have found that some business owners don't like their business being thought of as a hobby or nonprofit, although it effectively is. This conflict generally leads to the business not being able to achieve its financial goals and frustrates the owner significantly. The earlier you identify what is the actual purpose of your business, the better. This allows you to set appropriate goals and measures for achieving success. There's nothing wrong with having this type of business; if you understand that it shouldn't be measured in the same way as other types of businesses.

I run into some entrepreneurs who desire to start or have both a nonprofit and an enterprise together, or two enterprises concurrently. This is not a good strategy because it is hard enough to have one successful business at a time. It is critical to focus your efforts until the first one is running successfully before attempting a second. My recommendation is always to pick one, generally the for-profit. You can only help people from a position of strength, so get your business running successfully and finances in order before going the nonprofit route. Plus, in my opinion, there are way too many small underfunded nonprofit organizations out there and it's usually better to support existing nonprofits both financially and by volunteering. Most people don't realize that it is more difficult to start and run a nonprofit than a for-profit business.

The current economy is sometimes referred to as the "gig economy" because the number of freelancers and consultants has grown significantly due to corporate downsizing, businesses outsourcing to focus on their core competencies, and technology making it much easier to work from anywhere. In 2016, nearly 53 million Americans were freelancers; that's 34% of the workforce! Projections show that by 2020 43% of the U.S. workforce will be freelancers. For example, most graphic artists no longer work for a single company, but rather develop a group of clients that they support on a regular basis. These types of businesses tend to focus on providing a job for the entrepreneur, as opposed to seeking expansion to become an employer. There's nothing wrong with this type of business either. However, there are limitations on time, resources, and the ability to grow. The value and the scalability of this type of business is usually very limited.

"Focus on Becoming an Enterprise, able to function independently of the owner."

In my opinion, most businesses should be focused on becoming an enterprise to achieve the maximum value and level of business success. The goal of enterprises is to grow and become self-sustainable, and to eventually be able to function independently of the entrepreneur or business owner. Even the purpose of businesses with no employees can be enterprising based on the mission, vision, and plans. Businesses that start out in the other categories can eventually become enterprises as the owner expands his or her thinking and goals. Eventually, many self-employed business owners seek to become an enterprise as the owner bumps up against the limitations of self-employment such as time, not being able to sell, and lack of social interaction.

How would you categorize the purpose of your business?

SBPro® Business Purpose

Hobby

Nonprofit

Self-Employment

Enterprise

<u>Growth</u>

Most small business owners don't have a growth mind set; they're not thinking about growing, rather than just maintaining or surviving. Given the rapid state of change happening around us, standing still is equivalent to moving backward and getting left behind. As a business owner, you must focus on growing and achieve growth in many areas. The biggest area is growth in your knowledge and understanding of business. Because you are the leader of your business, nobody is more committed or has a greater impact on it than you. Small business owners must be prepared, knowledgeable, and capable of doing what is required. Your personal development and professional development is of the utmost importance. That's not to say you won't make mistakes, but hopefully they will be smaller mistakes, and you will learn more from them. Small business owners should be inquisitive and always learning. They should seek out the counsel of other business owners, organizational leaders, and advisers. At the end of the day, your business can only go as far as you are prepared to take it.

"Focus on growing revenue, profit, and capacity."

Business owners are responsible for setting organizational goals for performance. If there is not a focus on growing revenue, profitability, and capacity, it simply will not happen. To keep your business sustainable, you should have a plan in place to increase every year. Growing organizations provide opportunities for business owners and employees to develop professionally and stay engaged. Ultimately, expansion is necessary to create the business that you desire.

Initially, small business owners should focus on a small target market (niche). This allows them to concentrate on the people most likely to buy their products and services. As a business owner becomes more knowledgeable and the organizational capabilities and capacity increase, then he or she is ready to look at ways to grow their target market. Personal growth drives organizational growth and organizational growth drives target market growth.

SBPro® Growth Plan

Target
Market

Organizational

Personal

Journey

As an entrepreneur, there is a certain journey you must take if you desire to move your business to the next level. It starts with developing your product and/or service to ensure that there is a market for it. That is the first stage of <u>working IN your business</u>. This is when you are focused on product and service delivery as well as spending a lot of time working within the business. Usually, small business owners cannot go away without closing their business which causes them to lose income and revenue, since the business doesn't run as smoothly as when they are there. At a certain point, you must pivot away from primarily focusing on product and service delivery to take your business to the next level - working ON your business.

Once your products, customer base, and target market are established, it is time to begin working ON your business, rather than IN it. Now, what does that mean? The key to optimizing your business model is analyzing both quantitative and qualitative information to make better business decisions. The challenge for most small business owners is first knowing that this transition is needed and then understanding how to make it. Many small business owners never make it this far. However, by reading this book you'll be more prepared to optimize your business model. It involves creating, gathering and analyzing information to understand how your business really works, and building enough capacity to significantly expand. Then the business can run smoothly without you and then your focus should shift to working ON THE FUTURE of your business.

By creating a sustainable business model with processes and procedures, it is time to focus on planning to grow your business rapidly. This can be accomplished by expanding the target market, adding additional products, and horizontal or vertical integration. You must bring in additional expertise and develop a strong leadership team because few entrepreneurs possess all of the skills that they will need. It also involves doing research and analysis on your company, the market, your competition, and future trends to determine the best course of action.

Successfully completing this journey requires you to develop and evolve from working IN your business as a creator, employee, and supervisor to working ON your business as a manager; and then, ultimately <u>working ON THE FUTURE of your business</u> as a leader. This transformation is not easy to accomplish, and many business owners are not up for the challenge. However, knowing the path allows you to get the right type of assistance throughout the journey to accomplish your goals. My book *The Masterpreneur Playbook:* expands upon this journey in a "5-Step Business Growth Plan from Startup to Scaling Your Business."

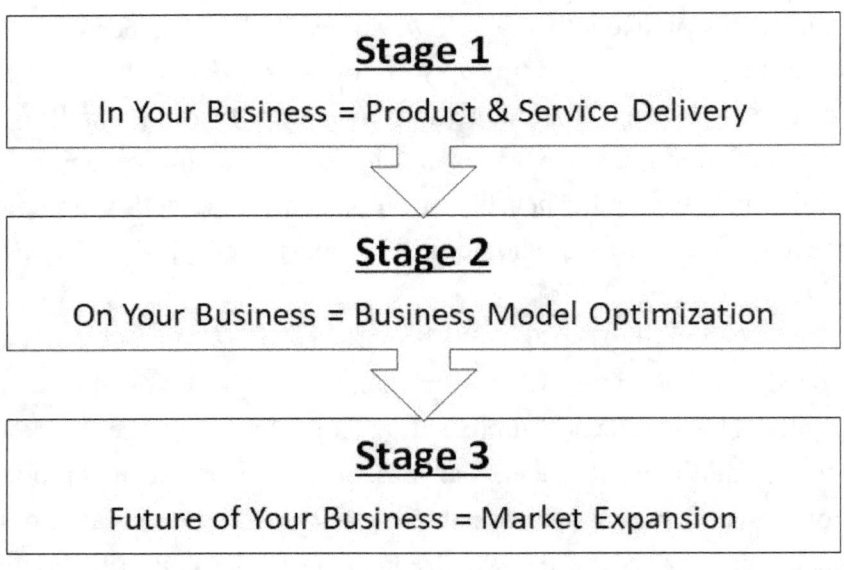

SBPro® Critical Path

Stage 1
In Your Business = Product & Service Delivery

Stage 2
On Your Business = Business Model Optimization

Stage 3
Future of Your Business = Market Expansion

Process

The key to running a successful business is making good business decisions. The key to making good business decisions is basing them on current, accurate information that is both quantitative and qualitative. The only way to do this is through creating processes and procedures for every aspect of your business. My SBPro Methodology outlines a three-step strategic planning process that will help you to obtain and process information to make the best possible decisions for growing your business.

Step 1: Assessment & Visualization - obtain an objective determination of where things currently stand and develop a clear picture of where you want to be.

Step 2: Analysis & Recommendations - involves examining the information obtained from Step 1, studying the environment, and exploring options to determine the best course of action.

Step 3: Implementation & Evaluation - putting your plans into action and measuring performance against metrics so that you can make regular adjustments to better achieve the results that you desire.

SBPro® Methodology

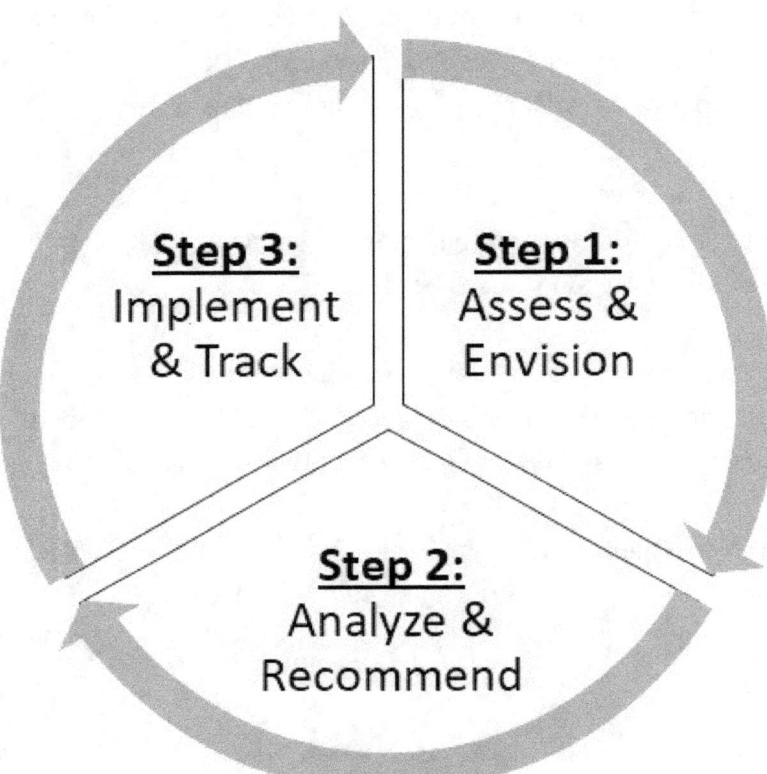

Learn more about topics discussed in this chapter from the workbook, my book *The Masterpreneur Playbook: How to Master Business Growth From Startup To Scaling* and courses available at the Small Business Pro University (www.SBProU.com).

Key Learnings

1) Be clear about why you are a small business owner and what benefits you seek.

2) Understand whether creating an enterprise is critical to achieving your goals.

3) Have and continually update a plan for growing your business knowledge, the capacity of your organization, and the markets you serve.

4) Follow the critical path of working IN your business (product and service delivery), then ON your business (business model optimization), and finally ON THE FUTURE of your business (market expansion).

5) Use the SBPro Methodology as your process for continual improvement.

Chapter 2 – What-Is My Most Important Job?

SALES AND MARKETING. Period. Don't ever let anyone tell you different. Yet, most entrepreneurs start their businesses without realizing it. You simply cannot be successful without the right priorities. So, as an entrepreneur, do you place your primary emphasis on developing your product? On strengthening and perfecting your customer service? On fine-tuning your finances? They're all important, but first things first - and that is clearly, sales and marketing. Without them, you have no business, plain and simple - no matter what industry you have chosen to go into.

"Without Sales and Marketing, You Have No Business."

Admittedly, to succeed as an entrepreneur requires a multitude of skill sets. Few, if any of us, have all of them. However, so many business owners start out by turning a hobby into a business or taking their craftsmanship from a previous job and seeking to turn that into a business. Many of you reading this went into business not thinking you would be doing sales and marketing (you went to school to become an electrician, right?). But, as a business owner, you simply have to do sales and marketing if you genuinely want to succeed - and you have to spend a lot of time doing it as well as learning how to do it well.

Once you understand this all-important tenet of business startup and growth, how do you go about it? It's all about asking the right, important questions. Many business owners learn how and continue to engage in effective, ongoing sales and marketing without expensive training. Often, they learned from experience by trying and failing miserably with their prior efforts.

<u>Marketing</u>

We could give you volumes on marketing. Instead, we will focus on just those key elements you absolutely need to know to market your business effectively. First, you need to think about your branding. On the big picture, once you have successfully embarked on product development, you will then proceed to create your organization, then optimize the business before seeking to expand into new markets. So, let's start by discussing your product or service. You must clearly define what your customer will receive in return for his or her investment in your product or service. Define exactly what you are selling, for what price, and precisely to whom you are selling it. Notice I said "precisely" as this is your target market. Most business owners simply think about this critical item in the wrong way, making it difficult to come up with a sound strategy to capture their share of the market by acquiring customers. If you learn nothing else, know this: as a small business, you have limited resources and limited capacity. Therefore, your strategy must be built on what you have to work with. That said, let's drill down and really define your target market as follows:

"Target Market Consists Solely of Your Most Likely Buyers"

1. Your target market consists solely of your most likely buyers. By defining it this way, you will spend less time and energy marketing to them because they are people who already see the value of your offering. They see your product or service as the solution to their problem, challenge, or need. Hint: you may have to approach different targets until you find the best one for you.

2. These are the people you can best market to effectively with the resources you have. You will therefore achieve your greatest success with a smaller group - a well-defined niche. This further allows you to position yourself as the best solution provider for their needs. Now it's time to ask yourself:

What is my value proposition? You need to show your potential customer that you understand what they need and can provide it. In truth, many customers may at some time, or another buy from you, but if you narrow your target to those most likely to buy, you will make the best investment of your time and your money; and in turn, get the best return on those investments.

Selling

Sales and marketing go hand in hand. They're different, but they are interdependent. You need to market your product or service in order to find customers and then sell it to them. With that in mind, let's talk about selling. Once again, you can and should learn as much about it as you can, but we're just going to give you a primer on those few critical items you need to know in order to get started. First, you have to know WHY people buy from you. It may not be the obvious reason. Maybe you don't have the best product or the best price, but they still may choose yours. Maybe they buy from you because they LIKE you, or because they like what you stand for.

Customer acquisition takes time and effort. Most often, people don't buy until the seventh touch. That means you have to connect with your prospective customer seven times before they will buy either by telephone, by email, in person ... whatever it takes. And you must spend both time and money to get those seven touches. Yes, it's sometimes hard to convert those likely buyers to customers, but it's a lot harder to convert those who are unlikely to buy. Like any other great and meaningful discipline, it's a process. It takes time and it takes patience.

How do you determine who are your likely buyers? Start by asking these questions: Who has the greatest need for what you have? How competitive are you and your products? Who will you make your best connection to? Hint: play to your strengths. Think about the various ways you can bring value beyond your core product and service that your competition can't. It's all about building a relationship with your customer that leads to TRUST. And that begins with you understanding their needs better than anyone else does. It may sound strange, but there are lessons here to learn from a drug dealer, in how he or she operates.

Market Your Business Like A Drug Dealer?

You need to market your small business like a drug dealer. Sounds crazy right? It does until you take a closer look at their marketing and sales strategy. Small business owners can learn a lot from analyzing what drug dealers do in terms of defining their target market, performing marketing activities, and building relationships.

Disclaimer: I do not encourage or condone the selling of drugs or anything associated with it. This is meant for educational and training purposes because of the clear examples and useful insights that can easily be understood by analyzing what they do. However, the drug business can be very lucrative, especially the ones that are legal.

Working with over 250 small business owners in many different industries, I have found that being able to market effectively is a significant challenge. Not necessarily because they don't want to, but because they may not understand how to do it. As part of my coaching, I tell my clients that they need to market their business like a drug dealer. Skepticism is not uncommon, but people always find this exercise valuable because it is a simple way to learn the three most important factors in marketing their small business more effectively.

1. Drug Dealers Do Not Try to Sell to Everyone

Have you ever been pressured to buy drugs from a drug dealer? No one I know that wasn't interested in drugs has ever been. Generally, drug dealers offer drugs rather than sell them because drugs sell themselves. The reason they sell themselves is because the dealers are talking directly to their target market and avoid wasting time with people who are not. The same principle works for small business owners.

Finding the right target market is one of the most important factors that contribute to the success of a business. Most small business owners have one of the following marketing challenges:

- They don't know that they need to have a target market.
- They don't really understand what a target market is.
- Their target market is too large to adequately service.

Many small businesses think the target market is anyone who might or is currently purchasing their product. However, they should really be focusing on the people who are most likely to buy their product or services. It must be an active strategy where the size is based on the amount of time, money, and resources that can be invested for marketing to prospects. This is generally a much smaller segment than they are considering. The goal is to be the big fish in a small pond, rather than a little fish in the big pond because little fish get eaten.

For example, one of my clients, Tina Tang, owner of Iron Strong Jewelry (www.IronStrongJewelry.com) has a business that creates jewelry to celebrate the fitness achievements of women. Tina originally targeted female buyers between 18 and 65 years old. That represents 91 million people in the United States, according to the 2010 US Census. As a small business, how could she ever expect to market to that many people effectively? After analyzing her customers and doing additional market research, she found the best market for her product is actually men who are seeking to purchase a special gift for their significant other. Who knew? That's approximately 60 million people - still a lot.

She further refined her target market to be married men between 30 and 50 years of age with an income of more than $100,000 living in the New York City metropolitan area (MSA – NY/NJ/CT/PA) which reduces it to 283,986 people, according to the 2010 US Census. Further reducing by targeting only men with wives who are mothers that work out and who search for their gifts online using Google® brings the target market to fewer than 14,199 people. That's a much more reasonably sized target market. By doing this, Tina not only reduces the scope of her marketing effort, she is also able to reach her prospects more effectively. It allows her to create focused content that clearly demonstrates her unique value proposition and deliver it through the most appropriate channels. This approach is much more effective in converting prospects into customers.

2. Drug Dealers Don't Pay for Marketing

Although drug dealers generally don't spend a lot of money on marketing and advertising, they are still able to run a very profitable business. They are extremely proficient at guerilla marketing, an advertising strategy that focuses on low-cost unconventional marketing tactics that yield maximum results. You can learn more about it in the book by the same title, authored by Jay Conrad Levinson. Given that small business owners often have very limited marketing budgets, their focus needs to be on free or low-cost marketing activities and maximizing every dollar they spend. To do this, they must know their customers extremely well and be able to identify with their needs.

Small business owners can be very successful without having a very expensive website or being a master at social media. Many small business owners overly focus their efforts on cutting edge websites and crazy social media strategies that they cannot afford, and which may not be consistent with reaching their target market.

3. Drug Dealers Make Friends

Drug dealers are laser focused on getting recurring business by building relationships with their clients, charging full price, and getting high margins, even though it's a commodity business. They know their customers, and more importantly, their customers know them, which results in repeat business and referrals. Drug dealers know the real reason clients buy from them and that is "because they like them." But without knowing you, how can they like you? What do your prospective clients know about you and your business?

Many entrepreneurs started their business because they were good at something or liked something, rather than to sell and to market, which is really their job. They can come across as insecure when they talk about their business. This detracts from their ability to connect with customers. Have you ever seen a drug dealer who was not confident about what he or she does? You, too, can become a master relationship builder by reading the book *How to Win Friends and Influence People* by Dale Carnegie and putting his simple, yet powerful principles to work.

In conclusion, a business can run without doing a lot of things, but marketing and selling is not one of them. As you can see, there is a lot that small business owners can learn from drug dealers! First, you need to define the right target market; second, you need to minimize your marketing and sales expenses; and third, you need to be good at building relationships. Your business will thrive if you incorporate these strategies effectively.

"Craft the Right Value Proposition and Find Those that See it."

Finding Your Target Market

So, what's the goal here? To craft the right value proposition and to find those that see it. Ultimately, that will prove to be a smaller, more manageable group. Therefore, you can communicate better with them and focus on the solution. Allow me to give you a real world example from my coaching experience with Angela Huggins. Sewing was one of the life skills she learned from her mom. It allowed her to be creative and since she loved dolls, Angela sewed a doll world. Making dolls allowed her to stoke her imagination through color, fabric, and books. If she couldn't find it in the store, she would create the dream doll dress, doll furniture, and/or doll house. Travelling from state to state meeting dollmakers, taking classes, and teaching others was therapeutic and brought her joy. Angela believes that dolls are magic and seeks to share the experience with others through her business, Angel Hugs 4 All.

When she came to me, Angela struggled to make enough sales. She sold dolls and viewed her target market as anyone who might buy one of her dolls. She was attempting to sell them at mainstream events attended by large numbers of people. We shifted her strategy. Instead, she found opportunities at doll shows. Far fewer people attended, yet her sales went up. Approaching the right market became both easier and more productive. Do the same and it will drive your business upward. Just figure out the right target market and focus on them.

There's a bonus in talking to your target market: sometimes they will also help you learn more about your product, so you can make changes in things like your sizes or quantities or your delivery methods, resulting in an enhanced product offering with a stronger value proposition. This is essentially free market research, so always take customer feedback whenever you can get it.

Since sales and marketing is one of the most critical aspects of your enterprise, it's worth your while to do additional research. See what other companies are doing to attract customers. Look at their colors, their designs, the type of people they interact with - even how their employees are dressed and how they communicate with their customers. Every time you do something as simple as go out to a retail store or to a restaurant, take a close look at how they are marketing themselves and learn from it. In short, you don't have to reinvent the wheel. Utilize others' best practices. Companies have spent millions of dollars to figure out how to do it right. They have proven ways, already established. Why not save time and money benefitting from what they have already done?

Branding

Let's talk about the "B" word - BRANDING. What is it really? Branding involves everything encompassing your overall product experience. It should tell a story and have a specific message. Branding is the emotional experience a customer has when he or she interacts with your company, your product, and your employees. It includes everything from your company name to your logo and identity to your colors. Your branding drives your strategy. Be authentic by representing what you and your business stand for. Be original, be different, be visible! Your branding differentiates you. It tells people why they should know about your business. When you own and operate a small business, you are your brand. As somebody once stated it: "Your smile is your logo, your personality is your business card, and how you leave others feeling is your trademark."

"Branding is the Emotional Experience A Customer Has When Interacting with Your Company"

Your experience and your expertise are your credibility in the marketplace. As a salesperson, how you speak, dress, and represent your business all matter. And no one can market and sell your business as well as you can because you are selling yourself. Let's make it tangible. When it comes to your brand, choosing your business's name is crucial. Your business's name can help you achieve what you are trying to do. To be successful, take this task seriously. Your business's name should help people understand what your business does. That said, make sure people can pronounce and spell it. Make it an attribute, not a detractor. Your online presence, visibility, and searchability is so important in today's world, you must be able to have your business name as your website domain name. If not, then change the name.

Since it is not always possible to say everything you want and need with your business name, your tagline becomes nearly as important. Your tagline continues to enhance the understanding of your business's name. We did this by adding to my business name "Small Business Like A Pro," which tells you that I work with entrepreneurs to improve their performance. Our tagline, "The More You Know, The Faster You Grow" lets people know we provide our clients with knowledge, as well as strategies to grow. It leaves no question about why people engage with us. Here's a few hints when creating yours:

- Your tagline must communicate quickly.
- Keep it professional.
- Make it appeal to your target customer.
- Keep it to 3-5 memorable words.
- Make it surprising, funny, and inventive.

Create a logo that reflects your business's brand. Many companies have spent a great deal of time, energy, and money on this important feature of their brand s identity. Your logo can become an important asset to your business, not only so customers will recognize your company, but it adds value at the time you may decide to sell your business. Here's a few hints for successful logo creation:

- Keep it simple.
- Keep it versatile so it adapts to different formats.
- Limit it to a few colors.
- Make it memorable.

- Make it appropriate for your target customer.
- Keep in mind that you can always update or refresh it.
- Once you have settled on a preliminary design, talk to your target customers and see how it resonates with them.

When we did our preliminary logo design, we had a football player running the ball with the Heisman Trophy pose, signifying "Running Your Small Business Like A Pro" (i.e. a pro, running). As much as I liked the concept, it did not resonate with any of the clients with which I shared it. We revised it with my secondary concept of 3 people celebrating a win, which everyone liked better. However, this version had two women on the sides and a man holding the trophy. Several of my female clients wondered why a woman wasn't in the middle holding the trophy. Since two-thirds of my clients are female, we put together a new version based on that feedback. However, in that version the woman being shorter than the men was an issue. Even small details are important. Fortunately, everyone liked the current version with three people celebrating the successful trophy win. Get your target market's perspective. After all, they are the ones paying you.

I also worked with Angela on her branding. When we started, she used the following:

- Title: Doll Maker
- Business Name: SewJC
- Tagline: NA
- Product: Dolls Starting at $50+
- Target Market: Anyone who might possibly like a doll
- Differentiation Strategy: Love of Dolls

After working with her on re-branding, she transitioned to the following:

- Title: Fabric Artist
- Business Name: Angel Hugs 4 All
- Tagline: Personalized Gifts and Heirlooms
- Product: Dolls $50+, Doll Pins $15, Paper Doll Making Kits $20, Paper Doll Making Contest Event $50.
- Target Market: White women aged 40-65 with a household income of $100,000; Doll Enthusiasts.
- Differentiation Strategy: Quality, customization, passion.

Which do you prefer and why?

Mission, Vision, and Core Values

One of the most important building blocks in the foundation of your business should be your MISSION, VISION, AND CORE VALUES. This is where you define what you are doing and why. They are not just statements or platitudes. Your entire mode of operating your business should be an outgrowth of these three overarching ideas. So, let's define them.

"Your Mission: Why Does Your Business Exist?"

Your mission statement defines why you exist. Let's take Starbucks® as an example. Look at the statement on the company's website. Starbucks exists to "inspire the human spirit, one person at a time." And you thought they just sold coffee. The mission is reflected in how their stores are decorated, and even the locations they have chosen. Starbucks' mission is important to both its customers and to its employees. It helps shape how employees approach achieving company goals and responding to customers. They use it as a context.

"Your Vision: What Your Business Will Become"

Your Vision helps you to see clearly what you want to achieve. It's your vision of what you want your business to become. As you define it, you become more successful. Once again, as an example, the vision to "to establish Starbucks as the premier purveyor of the finest coffee in the world while maintaining our uncompromising principles while we grow," has helped the company make better decisions.

Your core values are the basis for how your company makes decisions and how it interacts based on them. In the case of Starbucks, the company concentrates on issues like the environment and diversity. Values help them achieve their mission and maintain quality as well as satisfied, enthusiastic customers.

Developing Your Story

One final important piece of your marketing and branding involves telling your story. It's challenging for most business owners. That said, it's wise to seek the help of professionals to differentiate your business. It's all about articulating a solid value proposition for your potential customers. An article from *Entrepreneur* magazine comes to mind. Foodily described what they do as being the largest recipe aggregator, but that in itself is not a value proposition. When they hired a consultant, they then told their story as a company that gives you the opportunity to spend more time with your family and friends eating and enjoying meals at home. Hence, the new story of their business provided a solution and addressed a need or a desire for their target audience in a way that interested them. As a result, it created more of an opportunity for a connection to their potential customers. And that's what social media is all about.

Most people cannot tell their business's story concisely, even if they have been in business for years. In our sound bite world, this has become ever more important. To improve your marketing, create a sixty-second commercial about your business - even if you never air or publish it online. This will help you to clarify exactly what you are seeking to accomplish. It will help you to articulate your value proposition to your employees, to your customers, and even to potential investors. Creating this content is the most important thing you can do for your business. You will use this everywhere to market your business.

During our initial meeting I always ask clients to "Take sixty seconds and explain exactly what your business is about, and what you are trying to accomplish." I follow up by saying, "I want you to do it again. Please take another sixty seconds and tell me again." From there I ask, "Did the two stories match?" If not, that's a problem. First, it's critical that you have consistent content so that people will recognize that it's you in the marketplace. My second question is, "When you started, what was the first thing that you said? Were you talking about yourself, or were you communicating with your audience?" Your goal with the first five to ten seconds of any communication is to make a connection with your audience. Most people listen to the radio station WIIFM (What's In It For Me). Did you speak to their wants, needs, or desires? If not, you risked them shutting down and not really hearing what you are saying.

For example, if I said, "Hi, my name is Andrew Frazier, President and COO of Running Your Small Business Like a Pro, and I really love business. I graduated from MIT and went to business school at NYU. I used to be an officer in the Navy - blah, blah, blah ... would that make you want to listen?" However, if I said, "The key to small business success is generally to do the opposite of what large businesses do. As a result, many entrepreneurs and small business owners don't receive the guidance they need to achieve their goals. After working with more than 250 entrepreneurs and small business owners, I've seen many patterns and developed a methodology that will help them overcome obstacles and be more successful." Now, don't you want to hear the rest of what I have to say?" It's important to have a customer-centered approach to how you communicate about your business. In my humble opinion, this is one of the best ways to improve your marketing and selling success.

The SBPro Commercial Format

The key to creating a good commercial involves a four-step process, as follows:

Step 1: Create the Need - Use facts to create an emotional connection. Potential customers want to know that you understand what they need. By using facts, you can identify their problem or challenge and demonstrate an understanding of their specific need, want, or desire. In the case of life insurance, few people walk around thinking about purchasing it. Then, how are insurance agents able to get people to buy? They use facts such as having the person think about what happens when one member of a couple dies. "Have you ever been at a wake where the family had to pass the hat to cover the costs of the funeral?" After hearing that information, the person will think about life insurance as something that they may need.

Step 2: Introduce Your Solution - Explain your solution to address the challenge and explain what differentiates you from the competition. For example, again in the case of life insurance, the agent indicates that, "As an independent agent, I offer life insurance policies from all the major companies, ensuring that people get the best products and pricing possible."

Step 3: Provide an Example – Help the person visualize themselves benefitting from your solution through someone else's experience like, "My client, John Smith, passed away last month at the age of 42. During his family's time of need I brought his wife, Mary, a check for $1 million to maintain their lifestyle and ensure that the kids, Lisa and Tommy, can still go to college."

Step 4: Strong Close with Soft Ask – Open the door to start a conversation and develop a relationship with potential customers. For example, "While an unfortunate situation, think how much worse that would have been if John had not sat down with me and obtained the coverage he needed."

What your SBPro commercial format does not include: your name, your company name, an explanation of who you are. This is because it needs to be all about the potential client - not about you.

Let's debrief. What did the SBPro Commercial Format accomplish?

1. By creating the need, it let them know that you understand and care
2. Providing a solution lets them see what you know
3. Giving an example creates an emotional bond

4. The strong close with a soft ask helps determine if they are a good prospect

Imagine you were 45 years old with two kids in middle school and were mingling at a cocktail party. You introduce yourself to someone and ask what they do. They respond with…

"Have you ever been at a wake where the family had to pass the hat to cover the costs of the funeral? As an independent agent, I offer life insurance policies from all the major companies, ensuring that people get the best products and pricing possible. My client, John Smith, passed away last month at the age of 42. During his family's time of need I brought his wife, Mary, a check for $1 million to maintain their lifestyle and ensure that the kids, Lisa and Tommy, can still go to college. While an unfortunate situation, think how much worse that would have been if John had not sat down with me and obtained the coverage he needed."

In 30 seconds you probably went from not even thinking about life insurance to wondering if you have enough. How would you respond? Your response will be telling. The agent is seeking to qualify you as a prospect by seeking to start a conversation and gauge your interest. This gives him or her an opportunity to pre-sell, increasing the likelihood of obtaining an appointment and making a sale.

This is exactly the format most large companies use. They spend millions of dollars creating commercials for their products. You can learn a lot from watching their messaging and thinking about who they view as their target market and how they're trying to communicate. There is no shame in borrowing or stealing something you like and using it for your business. People do it all the time - even the large companies.

Learn more about topics discussed in this chapter from the workbook, my book *How To Sell More With Customer-Centric Marketing: Talk To Your Prospects, Not to Yourself,* and courses available at the Small Business Pro University (www.SBProU.com).

<u>Key Learnings</u>

1) Know that your most important job is to market and sell, which should be done for at least 2 hours daily.
2) It is important to continually improve your skills by training, practicing, and learning from what other businesses do.
3) The smaller and more narrowly defined your target market, the more success you will have.
4) Branding is proactively working to create the image you want others to have of your business.
5) People are not purchasing what you are selling, they are buying <u>what they believe you're selling does for them.</u> Focus on the customer and speak to their needs.

Chapter 3 – What Is My Greatest Fear?

There is Nothing to Fear but Fear Itself (F.D.R.)

For most small business owners and entrepreneurs, doing the numbers - really reviewing their costs, their sales, their margins - constitutes their greatest fear. Why? Because in so many cases, they are either not comfortable with math, they are not sure what to do, or they are simply afraid of the truth. Many small business owners go in to business with blinders on. You know, the "Don't confuse me with the facts" (Earl Landgrebe) mentality. They are experts at their craft, but they just may not have the financial chops. As a result, their biggest challenge is not using quantitative measures (numbers) and only using qualitative information (feelings) to manage their business.

Let's talk about fear for a moment. According to a survey by IFL Science, snakes, heights, spiders, and public speaking top the list of people's fears. So, are these and other fears just phobias - irrational fears with no basis in reality? In truth, it's reasonable to be afraid, but being afraid can be detrimental and make you miss important things. Let's revisit the fear of running your business by the numbers. That too is an irrational fear. Why do I say this? Because knowing your numbers can only help you. Most entrepreneurs and small business owners run their business by using qualitative analysis to make decisions. So-called "soft" or intuitive judgments may prove somewhat helpful, but they don't always give you the harsh reality of where your business actually sits on the success-failure scale. By ignoring the use of quantitative measures, you run the risk of making different decisions than you would have, had you understood the numbers associated with your choices. By using both qualitative *and* quantitative analysis in your decision making, you are better able to make the best decisions possible for your business success.

Remember the successful business person we told you about in the Preface? When asked how she became so successful, she indicated that she made good business decisions after learning from her bad decisions. Think about it. **What are two ways you learn in business?**

1. By taking the time to learn, study, and plan.
2. By losing money.

Which way would you prefer to learn?

"Taking the time to learn, study, and plan helps you to not lose money" of course.

Are you still afraid of doing your numbers? Just remember that it isn't rocket science. I want you to answer a few questions to better understand. Do you know how to count? Can you add numbers? What about subtract? Do you know how to multiply? How about divide? I know that sounds silly, but that's all it takes to be able to run your numbers. Fortunately, it's even easier than that because this is not a test of your math skills, so you can use a calculator to do everything. Therefore, your fear is irrational and there is **NO EXCUSE** for not doing your numbers.

Working ON Your Business

Let's examine a real-world example from my own experience. I was working with my client Myani Lawson, owner of

Envision Education. She started the Bergen Lafayette Montessori School (BLMS) in Jersey City, NJ. When we met, she was seeking to create the best educational experience possible for her students while doing it at a reasonable cost. There is certainly nothing wrong with that especially if you can do it and still stay in business. However, this strategy generally results in less income and greater costs, a recipe for disaster. Not surprisingly, Myani was having cash flow challenges like most small business owners, and she wasn't sure why. As an educator, it made sense to her to create the best educational experience without necessarily focusing on her operational costs. However, her tuition was less than all other Montessori schools in the area. In addition, items that other schools charged extra for, such as an organic lunch and activities like karate, dance, physical education, and Spanish language lessons, were included in BLMS tuition even though she brought other people in to provide those services, at a cost to her.

Ultimately, Myani went from being an educator who has a school to a business person who runs a school. This is exactly the transformation entrepreneurs need to make but find it very difficult to do so on their own. Those two perspectives would result in differing decisions. So, how did we get her to make the transition?

First, I had Myani read the *eMyth Revisited* by Michael Gerber. It is by far the best book for entrepreneurs and you are doing yourself a great disservice if you don't read it. The tag line says it all: *"Why Most Small Businesses Fail and What You Can Do About It."* What entrepreneur or business owner wouldn't want to know that? The book provided her perspective and knowledge about what it takes to succeed in business. Also, understanding the three competing personalities – technician, manager, and entrepreneur helped her better understand the voices in her head. In addition, Myani learned the importance of working ON her business rather than working IN it. Reading the book ignited her passion, which lead to the creation of a clearer vision for the future or her business. As a result, Myani became more open to change and willing to embrace the personal transformation necessary for her to succeed.

I worked to help Myani understand her business model from a quantitative perspective. When we reviewed her numbers, it clearly showed that her fixed costs were too high to be supported by the number of students she had. By doing that, we were able to start making decisions that would help her to improve that situation. However, this would never have happened if she wasn't willing to try something new, and if we hadn't run the numbers. We also determined that if this trend were to continue, she would be out of business within several months. The analysis also helped us to figure out how much she needed to cut expenses and determine the amount of additional funds she needed to raise. This allowed her to create a viable plan to move forward successfully and ensure that she does not end up in this situation again. Fortunately, Myani was able to obtain the financing to run her business effectively. We will discuss how in the next chapter, "Where Will I Find the Money?"

For the new year, I helped her put together the business model on a spreadsheet, so that she could do projections based on various assumptions. It allowed her to calculate how much her business could actually afford to spend on fixed costs, based on the number of students enrolled. We also looked at all the different expenses she had, in order to determine what she could do less expensively or eliminate altogether. We talked about strategies for increasing her enrollment, which would provide additional revenue to more effectively cover her costs and provide economies of scale. By increasing BLMS's top line revenue, it made each additional student more profitable to the school. There is no way the right decision could have been made had she not done the numbers. I am happy to report that BLMS is currently in business, profitable, and thriving with twice as many students. Myani has hired additional teachers and a full-time head of school, freeing her up to focus on market expansion and growth. She is currently leading the efforts to establish a Montessori public charter school in Jersey City to provide continuity for graduates of her program. It will also provide greater access for other students whose families cannot afford a private school Montessori education.

Most small businesses simply do not correctly anticipate their startup costs. They don't put together a thorough plan to determine what they need. As a result, they start out undercapitalized and can never catch up. hold to seek additional capital. Most businesses can often start on a much smaller scale than where the So, what should they do? They need to either change their plan, so they don't need as much money, or put the project on entrepreneur thinks they should.

Many entrepreneurs ask questions like: Which numbers are you talking about anyway? Where do you get them? What should you do with them? And how does this help your business? We'll explore that next.

Getting the Numbers

There are four primary categories of numbers that you must have and various sources for finding the specific numbers that should be used.

First, you need to be aware of your cash balance and cash flow information on a daily basis. This information is found in your online banking portal and monthly bank statements.

Second, you should know your revenues or sales on a daily, weekly, monthly, quarterly, year-to-date, and/or an annual basis, as appropriate for the size and type of business you have. It is not enough for your accountant to have them or say that they are in the point of service (POS) system. You must review and know them yourself! This is not something that you can delegate. This information can be pulled from your POS system, book keeping software, sales tracking spreadsheet, ledger book, and/or daily reports.

"You Must Know Your Sales & Costs - Do NOT Delegate This"

Third, you need to know how much it costs to deliver your product or service (variable costs). Not what you think it costs, but what it really costs! This includes any sales workers, and/or people directly delivering the services. Variable costs only increase as a result of obtaining additional revenues. This distinction is a very important item when it comes time to analyze your numbers and calculate break-even sales.

Last but not least, are expenses that commissions, materials, freightshipping, production

are incurred even if you don't make any sales (fixed costs). Your fixed costs include rent, utilities, insurance, marketing, and employees (except for those involved in creating your products and those delivering your services directly, which would be variable costs).

Organizing the Numbers

Once you have obtained the right numbers, the next step is to organize them into financial statements, a more usable format. The three main financial statements that small businesses use are:

:

1) **Balance Sheet** – tells the financial position of the business at a single point in time like a personal net worth statement.

2) **Income Statement** – tells how much money the business made by subtracting expenses (fixed and variable) from revenues (sales). Also, known as the Profit & Loss (P&L) or business model.

3) **Cash Flow Statement** - shows incomings and outgoings of cash, representing the operating activities of an organization. Since income (profit) is not representative of how much cash you have, the Cash Flow Statement is used to make sure that you don't run out of cash and go bankrupt.

We will primarily focus on the business model (i.e. income statement or P&L) for the purposes of this chapter. The key is categorizing the fixed and variable costs as thoroughly and accurately as possible. Take a look at the simplified business model formula below.

SBPro® Business Model		
(i.e. Income Statement or P&L)		
Revenue	+	
Variable Expenses (COGS)	-	
Gross Profit	=	
Fixed Expenses	-	
Profit	=	

Using the Numbers

Financial statements make it much easier to both understand and manipulate the numbers. A lot of additional information about your business can be learned by analyzing the financial statements. You can identify trends by doing horizontal analysis (categories from period to period) and understand how different items have changed over time. You can also use vertical analysis (category to category in same period) to compare the relationship of different items to total sales or assets for the business. In addition, financial ratios allow you to effectively compare information with your company to other companies, industry averages, and/or different standards (apples to apples) to better evaluate information.

Developing and analyzing the business model allows you to better understand how your business works to create projections, do breakeven calculations, and test various scenarios for planning purposes.

After getting, organizing, and using her numbers, Myani was able to develop a plan to move her business forward successfully. She better understood how BLMS really worked so that she could make better decisions. She also developed a business model spreadsheet where she could easily test different assumptions, try various scenarios, and adjust numbers whenever additional information became available. This empowered her to optimize her business model and develop SMART (Specific Measurable Achievable Relevant Timebound) goals.

Myani started with the top line of the business model where the goal is to increase sales (revenues). She considered whether it should be done by increasing revenues from current customers and/or generating revenue from new customers. Myani chose to pursue new customers since her mission is to make a Montessori education affordable to as many as possible. She developed a plan to accomplish this goal through increased marketing investment, greater community outreach, and adding virtual information sessions, making it easier for more potential customers to learn about the school. Based on her Business Model, increasing revenues will have the greatest positive impact on profitability.

Since we calculated the marginal cost of adding an additional student, Myani knew the minimum amount she could charge without losing money. She came up with two creative ways to increase revenue from customers that would have otherwise been turned away for lack of funds and further support the school's mission. First, BLMS became part of the Urban League's voucher program. Even though the program has a low payout rate, it is still above the marginal cost of adding a student. Also, she developed a scholarship program that made the school more affordable and resulted in additional applications. Both of these programs had positive PR and marketing benefits in addition to boosting revenues and net income.

Then moving to variable costs, we want to incrementally decrease the overall variable cost factor per student. Myani looked at each component of variable cost to determine what impact they each had. As a service business, BLMS already had low variable costs. However, there was room to negotiate better per student pricing for certain activities and eliminate others currently being offered on a per student basis by external vendors. She also considered minor adjustments to the lunch program to reduce costs.

Gross profit is just the difference between revenues (sales) and variable costs (COGS). There is nothing additional we can do to directly improve it.

As a service business, the majority of BLMS costs are fixed, which we seek to minimize without negatively impacting the business. We looked at everything to see what could be done. Since rent was a large expense, Myani negotiated a slight discount from her landlord. Staffing is the single biggest cost, taking up more than half of her budget. She was able to adjust the schedules and fill in a few hours personally to change a teaching assistant position from full to part-time. At the same time, the BLMS marketing budget was expanded to grow enrollment and increase the number of students. Finally, she did eliminate a couple more outside vendors, replacing their activities with ones by staff members at no additional cost beyond their current compensation.

By making these decisions Myani was able to optimize her business model and maximize profitability while maintaining high standards at BLMS. Most importantly, she now has a sustainable business model which will allow her business to continue and grow profitably.

This proves that a whole lot can be done to proactively improve your business's financial performance by modeling it and making better decisions with the information it provides. By approaching decisions from a business perspective, Myani was able to grow revenues, decrease costs, and maximize the profitability of BLMS while fulfilling her mission of making a high-quality Montessori education available to a greater number of students. Plus, she is now able to work "ON" her business and take it to the next level.

Cash is King & Queen

Profit (Income) is not the same as cash flow. Which is most important? Well, you can have negative profits and still stay in business. However, when your cash balance is negative, you must add additional capital (funds) or your business is over.

Many business owners get themselves into trouble by assuming that their company's available cash will go up by as much as their profits. Unfortunately, it is a lot more complex. Just because your company made a profit doesn't necessarily mean that your cash increased. Therefore, your company can run out of cash by growing too fast as easily as it can from not having enough sales to cover expenses. How is this possible?

It is easy to understand how your company can run out of cash if it is losing money but running out of cash when your sales and profits are growing does not make sense at first glance. However, it requires an investment in marketing to achieve higher sales, it takes money to build additional capacity, and it takes cash to purchase additional inventory. This will cause a drain on cash in advance of realizing additional cash inflows from the growth in sales and profitability.

Profit = Sales – Expenses (Excluding Asset Purchases)

Cash Flow = Cash Inflows – Cash Outflows

One of my clients, Andy Vieira, CEO of Trucktech Parts and Services, learned this lesson the hard way. Andy grew up in Brazil and loved working on trucks and heavy equipment in the hot sun. The dirtier and grimier the job was, the more he liked it. Fast forward to coming to America and being an independent truck driver. Since other drivers always wanted him to repair their trucks, he ended up setting up a mobile truck repair business. From there, he opened a small parts store, then a single bay repair shop, and now he owns a multi-million-dollar business in the Ironbound section of Newark, NJ. He recently completed the Goldman Sachs 10k Small

Businesses training and is in the process of opening a paint spray booth for trucks as part of the growth plan that he developed.

Andy was perplexed by how his company grew by 20% and made a lot of profits, but he could not figure out where the money went. What was even worse is that he incurred a hefty tax bill and didn't have the money to pay it. How did this happen?

We will explore what happened by looking at his numbers (fictional numbers are used below for instructional purposes and to simplify the example). Let's start by looking at his income statement for the year…

Income Statement (P&L) 201x				
REVENUE	**+**	**$1 Million**	**100%**	**Sales**
Variable Cost (COGS)	-	$500k	50%	Costs directly related to sales
Gross Profit	**=**	**$500k**	**50%**	
Fixed Expenses	-	$300k	30%	Costs incurred w/or w/out sales
Operating Profit	**=**	**$200k**	**20%**	

Now let's look at his cash flow statement to see what happened to the profits…

Cash Flow Statement 201x			
Profit	+	**$200k**	Pre-Tax Profit
Equipment Purchase	-	$75k	Fixed Asset Purchase Non-Expense
Additional Inventory	-	$50k	Current Asset Purchase Non-Expense
A/R Increase	-	$35k	Accounts Receivable Credit to Customers
Loan Principle	-	$25k	Paydown Loan Balance
Owner Draw	-	$25k	Taking Cash for Personal Use
A/P Increase	+	$10k	Credit to You from Suppliers
Net Cash Flow	=	**$0**	**Change in Cash during the Year**

Even though the business made $200k in profits its cash balance stayed the same as when the year started because there was $200k in non-expense cash outflows. Plus, Andy now has a tax bill of $50k. Fortunately, he had excellent credit and the company was profitable. As a result, he was able to quickly secure financing to cover the shortfall. This saved him from incurring significant fines from the IRS and a potential lien on his personal credit. Many entrepreneurs in similar situations are not so fortunate. We will discuss how he was able to access capital for this situation and other business purposes in the next chapter.

Learn more about topics discussed in this chapter from the workbook and courses available at the Small Business Pro University (www.SBProU.com).

Key Learnings

1) Doing the numbers is not as scary as it seems.
2) You can't understand your business if you don't understand the numbers.
3) Without numbers you end up working "**IN**" rather than "**ON**" your business.
4) The numbers help you to plan more effectively and anticipate problems.
5) Waiting will only cost you more money (i.e. good decisions vs. learning from bad decisions).

Chapter 4 – Where Will I Find the Money?

One of the most famous phrases ever to come out of a Hollywood film and become a popular soundbite: "Show me the money!" Access to capital is one of the biggest challenges that many entrepreneurs and small business owners have. There are many reasons why it can be very difficult - from finding the right source, to creating a compelling enough business plan, to having enough of your own equity in the deal, to your own personal creditworthiness, to the viability of your product or service, as well as your qualifications to run the enterprise. Most people who have never sought financing usually have unrealistic expectations about attracting funding, which is why most deals just don't get financed. These expectations can come from hearing about glamorous, flavor-of-the-month private equity and venture capital investments, believing that your product is unique and will sell itself, and/or media and film glorifications that make it seem much easier than it really is.

Know this: the days of the napkin plans are over when you could jot down a few notes and walk away with a check for your enterprise. Since the financial crisis of 2008, it has become much harder to get any business financing and the amount of documentation, planning, and preparedness is much higher than it had been in the past. Some reasons why most small businesses seeking financing don't get it are as follows:

- Not knowing how much capital is needed
- Inadequate personal cash investment
- Business model doesn't work
- Not enough cash flow to support payments

- Sourcing from the wrong places
- Lack of preparation
- Failure to address credit issues
- Substandard business plan
- Incomplete financial projections
- Don't have right team / experience to succeed

The biggest failure is often an actual lack of knowledge about how their business works. That is evidenced by them not knowing their business model and not working on their business, which we focused on in the previous chapter.

Some people think that there are grants out there for small businesses. The truth is, there are no grants for all intents and purposes. The only viable way to get free money for your business is through business plan and pitch competitions, or possibly through crowd funding. However, they still require your time and energy, which has a cost. Crowd funding is much more difficult than it seems and yields much lower results than people realize. According to data from Quora, the distribution of Kickstarter campaign raise amounts is as follows:

- About 11% raise nothing at all (Indiegogo 14%)
- About 75% raise something < $10,000 (Indiegogo 81%)
- About 13% raise $10,000 to $100,000 (Indiegogo 5%)
- About 1% raise over $100,000 (Indiegogo 0%)

According to Kickstarter's stats page, only about 36% of Kickstarter campaigns succeed and, of those successful campaigns, the majority ended up with less than $10,000. If you want to raise a LOT of money, then you'll need an exceptionally desirable product-and-price, a highly persuasive page, and some great marketing to invite people to view your page, in that order. Also, it doesn't hurt to have a large network of wealthy people from which to draw.

Perhaps even more important, so many entrepreneurs under estimate the personal contribution that they need to provide, which is generally 30% or more. Think about that for a moment. Let's put this in real world numbers. If your start-up costs are $100,000, you'll need to bring $30,000 in personal funds to the table.

P.R.A.Y. for Financing

When I work with entrepreneurs and small business owners, I find that obtaining financing is one of their biggest challenges. Partially because it's more difficult than it used to be to obtain financing as a small business, but even more so, because they have not done what they needed to do to ensure that they were in the best possible position to get financing. As a result, I came up with the following methodology for helping prepare them to be as successful as possible at gaining access to capital.

As an entrepreneur or small business owner, you must **P.R.A.Y.** to obtain capital. Not necessarily meaning you have to get on your knees and pray, even though that doesn't hurt, but I'm talking about **P** for prepare yourself and your business; **R** for research the types of financing and types of lenders and investors to determine what is the best fit for your needs; **A** for assemble all the documents you need quickly and accurately; **Y** for yield, meaning being patient and allowing the lender or investor to drive the process as well as being flexible enough to respond to their needs quickly and effectively. As a small business owner, if you follow this 4- step process, you will be much more likely to obtain the right type of financing for your business. But not only that, the process will help you learn a whole lot more about how your business has worked, is working, and possibly impact your strategies for the future in a positive way.

First and most importantly, when should you start preparing for financing? Yesterday, if not sooner because the sooner you start, the better position you will be in when the time comes. Generally, you want to start planning to seek financing six months before you need it. This can seem like an eternity for many entrepreneurs and small business owners who want or need financing soon. Unfortunately, most business owners do not start seeking financing until it's almost too late often times making it even worse as they aren't really prepared or organized when they are trying to obtain it. As a result, they are denied, which negatively impacts their business.

Prepare

Let's start with preparing yourself and your business for financing. So, how do you prepare before going out to seek financing for your business? This involves doing an assessment of where things currently stand in terms of getting a copy of your credit report and knowing your credit score on the personal side, figuring out your net worth (assets minus liabilities), ensuring your tax returns are completed, your professional resume, your disposable income (income minus expenses), and other key items which will be evaluated during the financial decision making process.

I run into a lot of entrepreneurs who haven't looked at their credit report or seen their credit score in a while. They should regularly be checking these things, which can be done at www.freecreditreport.com or any of the credit bureau websites (Experian, Equifax, and TransUnion). It's not uncommon for there to be inaccuracies or minor issues that can easily be resolved. However, it may take two or three months for the changes to be reflected in their score. As a result, this needs to be continuously reviewed and updated to ensure it is as accurate as possible. Sometimes business owners think that their business credit history can be provided instead of their personal credit, which is totally false. Generally, your personal credit score is a key driver until you become a middle market business (revenues of $20 million annually).

It's important for you to also have a clear picture of your net worth, which shows how your assets compare with your liabilities. It also lists the various types of collateral that you might have. It is very possible for someone to have a negative net worth in that they owe more money than the value of everything they own. This is very common with recent college graduates, who have a lot of loans, but haven't had an opportunity to build up their assets. Having a negative net worth detracts from your ability to obtain financing, so it's important to know where you stand and seek to continually increase your personal net worth. The higher it is, the better.

It always surprises me how many business owners are behind in submitting their personal tax returns. Not necessarily behind on the most recent year, but multiple years, and some ever since the business started. Without having current tax returns filed, it's almost impossible to obtain financing. One, because that's the key document that lenders and investors use to analyze your profitability. This is due to the fact that it's very rare for people to overstate their personal income and pay more taxes than they need to. If you understate your income, that could negatively impact whether you obtain financing and will affect the total amount of financing you could be eligible to receive. At the end of the day, you need to submit your taxes and report the income as accurately as possible.

While you're preparing yourself personally, you also need to prepare your business, which involves keeping your financials up to date, preparing your business plan, your financial projections, and your business tax returns. Despite all business owners knowing they should have a business plan, most do not have one – or at least a current one. When seeking financing, any investor or lender will need to see your business plan to know how you plan to invest the capital and the expected return. Business plans also demonstrate how well you understand the business that you are in and serves as a guide to ensure that you stay on track with your goals. Your business plan does not need to be fifty or a hundred pages long. Lenders generally prefer a 1-3 page summary of the business and your growth plans along with financial projections. Sometimes they will want more, but most times that is enough if you are an existing business. (Check out *My Business Plan Workbook* by Laurana Edwards for a simplified way to create a good business plan quickly.)

As we talked about in the previous chapter, many small business owners do not use quantitative financial information when making business decisions. However, that is the only way to really understand how your business works and how it's doing. Like we discussed, it is your responsibility as a business owner to know and to understand your numbers, which goes a long way towards demonstrating that you can make good business decisions. As a result, you should always have current financial information and understand what it is telling you - either on a weekly or a monthly basis, depending on the type and the size of your business.

Once you have your personal and business information prepared, it is key to figure out how much money you need to start and to run your business, and what you need it for, as well as how you plan to obtain it - and how and when you plan to repay it. Most of the entrepreneurs and small business owners I have worked with tend to either significantly over or under estimate how much money they should be seeking. First, it's usually best to get what you need to cover your requirements for approximately 12 months, rather than all the money you think you will ever need. Second, it's important to do the work to figure out what you will spend it on in detail, as opposed to just throwing out a number, like $50,000, $100,000, or a million dollars.

If you're like most entrepreneurs, you're anxious to get out of the starting gate and onto the launch pad. That said, don't fall into the trap of shorting yourself on your capital requirements. Many times, people will significantly under estimate what they need because of not coming up with all their startup costs, over estimating their sales in the beginning, not really knowing their product costs, and minimum order amounts. But the biggest reason for under estimating is not including at least three months of fixed expenses as working capital. You need to add up your costs in as much detail as possible, and then add those three months of projected fixed expenses for your business. We learned about fixed expenses in the last chapter. As a reminder, these are expenses you will incur regardless of whether you make any sales.

When I first met Andy Vieira, CEO of Trucktech Parts and Services, who was introduced in the previous chapter, he was seeking counseling assistance with refinancing his facility through the Small Business Development Center (SBDC) at Rutgers Newark. He had acquired the building previously through seller financing, but this was his first time seeking bank financing. While assessing his preparedness, I found that his current tax return was on extension and his previous one return showed very little income. Also, his financial records were not as current and accurate as they needed to be. Due to this, Andy did not know enough about his business financially and was not yet ready to meet with potential lenders.

Andy was unhappy with his accountant who was having some health issues and was closing in on retirement. His accountant was very slow following up with information and became unresponsive. The accountant also didn't make any effort to train Andy's bookkeeper and share any financial knowledge beyond just delivering the tax return. Much like most accountants, his focus was on minimizing taxes which can be detrimental for companies seeking financing or wanting to sell in the next couple of years, since the tax return will show minimal income.

Tell your accountant in advance if you are seeking financing

We addressed Andy's preparation needs by bringing in a new bookkeeper/accountant to help get his financial records in order and to prepare his taxes. This also included amending his taxes from the previous year and onsite Quickbooks training for his internal bookkeeper. In addition, I helped Andy understand what his business model was saying about the company. We looked at his potential for financing and the impact it would have on the business. Trucktech's financial reporting and books are now up-to-date such that Andy reviews his financial statements on a weekly basis. This preparation was instrumental in Andy easily securing additional financing to implement the GS 10k Small Business growth plan he developed.

Research

R is for researching the various lenders, investors, and products to determine the best fit for your needs. Just like the social media landscape, where there are thousands of different online businesses and communities, the same is true for the financing world. Lenders and investors generally have a profile of the types of deals they prefer to do based on industry, company size, type of funding, and many other parameters.

It's also key to figure out which sources of capital are a good fit for your needs. Lenders and investors have different criteria, different preferences for types of businesses they will fund, have a certain range of how much they are willing to fund, and different expectations for repayment or return on investment. So, it's important to do some research or get assistance in determining this before you approach a funding source. We call it "fishing in the right pond." Some of the more common sources of financing fit these types of profiles:

Personal Investment - This is always the first and most important step in the financing process. No one is going to give you any money for your business if you're not investing in it yourself. Plus, personal savings is the best way to go if it's possible because there are no strings attached. Simply put, when it's your money; you're in charge. Also, you don't have to go through a time-consuming and draining process, so that you can focus all your energy on making the business successful. One problem with self-funding can be that you don't necessarily have an external perspective on the viability of what you are trying to do. It's easier - and more painful to learn a lot by losing your own money. Make sure not to spend all your money before getting financing!

Let's look at another typical funding source for startups. Most entrepreneurs use personal credit as a source of financing for their business at one time or another. This can be good or bad, depending on the situation. However, sometimes it becomes your only alternative. It can be good because it's quicker and easier to access and generally costs less than external financing sources. Finally, consider that using it may lower your credit score, depending on how much is used and how diligent you are in repaying it.

Friends and family – They may invest in you because they like or know you. However, it's very important to clearly outline what type of investment it is right up front to them; whether it is a loan versus a share of equity in your business, their expected return (minimal or market based), the time frame for getting their money back, and how to handle any disputes. This is one of the typical investments for many startups and early stage companies that are not making a reasonable profit.

In the previous chapter my experience working with Myani Lawson, owner of Envisions Education, uncovered her need for financing to get her cash flow situation back on track. Given the minimal profits her business had been generating and a lack of collateral, it would be very difficult to obtain bank financing. An SBA loan might have been possible, except that she and her husband were unwilling to use their home for collateral. That left only three financing options: personal savings, personal credit, or a friends and/or family investment. Since Myani had already exhausted much of her savings and personal credit, financing from friends and family was most practical. She put together a detailed proposal of her business plans and began presenting it to friends and family. Fortunately, she connected with someone who really identified with her school's mission and loaned her the funds that she needed at a reasonable rate with flexible terms. Doing the research helped her to not waste time pursuing financing from organizations that would not do anything for her because she did not meet their lending criteria.

Microlender – This option is best for loans of $10,000 or less, but many can go as high as $25,000 or $50,000. These lenders focus on businesses that cannot get traditional bank financing. The principal advantage to working with them is that they can be more lenient in certain ways. However, you still need to have sufficient income to pay back the loan and the rates are somewhat higher than a traditional bank. They like, but don't always require collateral. The good news is that there is a wider range of collateral types they are willing to use such as used cars or low cost business equipment. These lenders are usually nonprofits, but sometimes they are for-profit companies. Their general payback time frame is 5 years or less and interest rates may be 8-12% at this writing. Microlenders primarily fund businesses that may have something negative in their profile. They are willing to take the time to investigate and still consider them. Other lenders are most often unwilling to overlook those negative items which may include a past bankruptcy or legal issues. Many microlenders provide technical assistance to help entrepreneurs improve their credit and business skills in order to prepare them to qualify for bank financing in the future.

Cash-Flow Lenders - will finance you based on the cash flow going into and out of your business. There are significant negatives to using this type of financing that you should be aware of before signing on. For example, many of them charge high interest rates and deduct money from your account every day. Plus, they charge all of the interest up front so you have to pay off interest for the whole amount borrowed before you start paying any principal, which makes the cost even higher if you pay off the loan early. These are predatory lenders and you want to avoid them. However, some business owners get stuck with no other alternatives and turn to this type of financing as a last resort. It's helpful in the beginning. However, it often leaves them in worse shape or out of business before long. Generally, they will lend up to about 10% of the cash flow in your business.

Trade Credit - This involves getting payment terms from your suppliers so that you don't have to pay them C.O.D. Generally, you can get net 15 or 30 days to pay if your credit is decent and you haven't missed any payments to them. This is actually the easiest and best type of financing to get because the supplier is effectively lending you money at no cost to you.

Factoring (AR & PO) - Accounts receivable is the opposite of the above type of funding, where you are lending your customers at no cost, which strains your cash flow. However, there are sources for borrowing against your Accounts Receivable (factoring) in certain situations. However, you'll need to be working with a credit worthy customer, and you'll have to deliver your product or service in full with an approved invoice before you'll have access to the funds. This is generally best when working with larger companies and governmental institutions who may take 45-60-90 days before they pay you on an invoice. Instead, you are turning your receivables into cash much quicker. One advantage to this type of financing is that it doesn't create a debt you need to repay. However, you also need to have high enough margins (at least 25%) to ensure that you can afford to do it and remain profitable. It is neither the least nor the most expensive type of financing. A couple of other pluses to using this method of financing: rates go down the longer you have been doing it successfully, you don't have to re-qualify to get additional funds, and it is not necessarily based on your income, collateral, or credit profile.

Traditional Banking – These lenders range from Commercial/Community/Savings/Investment/Merchant/Private Banks to Credit Unions. Their products include: SBA Loans, Lines of Credit, Credit Cards, Mortgages, and Equipment Financing. Once we were able to help Andy prepare his financial information appropriately, it was time to explore his financing options.

Trucktech's double digit growth rate, good profitability, strong cash flow, and building collateral positioned him as bankable. The next step was finding the right lender that would provide him with great terms and a quick turnaround. His business was a better fit for small to medium sized banks because they like lending on real estate collateral and his sized company is their target market. Although he was a great candidate for financing, that doesn't ensure a fast closing. The process of obtaining underwriter approval, completing an environmental report and appraisal on the property, and providing numerous documents, it still took around 60 days to gain access to the funds. Due to the amount of real estate equity, Andy was able to secure a mortgage loan, a significant credit line, and equipment financing all at once. He was also able to get great rates and negotiate the fees down to almost nothing. It is tough to qualify for regular bank financing, but the terms and fees are so much lower than most other options.

Angel Investors - Yes, there are angels among us, here on earth. Who are they? These are private individuals and groups of people that have pooled their money and like to invest in promising startup and early stage businesses. Although angel investors seem like a great source, it is rare to get money that way unless they happen to be your own friends and family. Just know that they will require a strong business plan and a marketable product. A strong management team is essential. They place a great deal of weight on the likelihood of the team's ability to implement the plan successfully when they look at a potential funding deal. Angel investors tend to invest in industries they understand. Therefore, your business must fit within the scope of what they tend to fund, so do your research before approaching them. They also prefer to invest in local businesses they can keep an eye on. Some individual angels invest from $25,000 – $250,000. Some groups will syndicate and fund up to $1 million. However, most small businesses simply do not fit their profile. They see tons of deals and only a very few get funded. So, what are your chances with these investors? See if your business meets these additional criteria: they are looking for businesses with a high growth rate and a fairly quick exit opportunity (generally18-36 months). They don't want to be your lifelong partners. They just want to successfully get you off the launch pad, up to profitability quickly, and generally see your business then move on for future rounds of expansion capital provided by Venture Capital or Private Equity investors. Angel investors usually seek at least a 20% return. Most don't provide additional assistance besides the money, but some individuals might. However, they'll usually let you run your business without much interference.

Venture Capital (VC) - Also known as "Vulture Capital" because of the way some VC's tend to operate. Even though the allure of getting this type of investment is strong, it's extremely difficult to obtain and there are many strings attached. You should know that the VC's become intimately involved with you in running the company, and they set up many progressive milestones for the business to achieve and will take additional equity (ownership) if they are not met. Many of them insist on a majority stake themselves, or for the syndicate. This means you risk becoming a minority shareholder of the business you started - what we commonly refer to as "dilution." VC's also have very high revenue expectations and seek to earn at least 100% annualized on their investments over a five year period. Therefore, companies they invest in will need to achieve exponential growth for them to even be interested. They do provide a depth of experience and connections, however. Typically, VC's are attracted to these sectors: technology, healthcare, media and entertainment which are all businesses that have high margins and are scalable. Please note that you will have to pay them up front for their due diligence fees to investigate and explore the viability of your business before they will take your deal. VC's mostly consider investments of at least $10 million.

Private Equity – Private equity investment is also difficult to obtain because these firms generally require a business to be profitable with a proven product or service and the potential to grow significantly. They prefer to take less risk than VC's, but still need to have a return of at least 25% annually on their money. Private equity investors will stay in with a longer time horizon than VC's; generally, they are more patient. However, in order to secure their interest and their funding, you will need a compelling story, a strong management team, a strong business plan, and significant growth potential.

Assemble the Information

Once you have prepared yourself and your business and researched the type of financing you are seeking and the best potential lenders and/or investors, it is time to assemble the information that they will need. If you have ever purchased a house, you know about all the documents required and additional requests you have to provide. For business financing, there are way more requirements, so it's important to get started putting them together before you need them. Most times, there is a standard document list of what they want from you. It includes three years of personal and business tax returns, year to date financial statements, as well as the last two years, your personal financial statements and accounts receivable aging report, a debt schedule, and a business plan or company summary. Beyond that, there are many additional items that may be requested up front or throughout the under writing process. The quicker you provide the requested documents, the faster your applications will be processed and the more comfortable the lender or investor will be with you. Some of these other items include your driver's license, bank statements, sales by customer, company formation documents, listing of equipment, accounts payable aging report, your bio, resume, certification, agreements and contracts with references, and account/attorney information. Assembling this in advance reduces stress and helps to ensure that you are providing accurate information on a timely basis, which speeds up the process. Generally, you should have these in an electronic format, so you can email or upload them quickly upon request.

Yield

The last part is the most difficult because you must yield to under writers and analysts, since you will have very little control over what happens from there. Sometimes it can be frustrating, especially as they keep requesting more and more documents when they could have asked for everything up front. It's even worse when they ask you for the same thing repeatedly. This process can feel like Chinese water torture where they would drip water on your forehead until it drives you insane! Despite how painful the process may be, it eventually ends when you will either be approved for financing or need to regroup and find another way. Even after being approved, it doesn't necessarily mean that you will close and have access to capital. Your deal can fall apart anywhere up until you have the money in your bank account, which can seem like forever, especially when you really need the money. However, there generally isn't anything you can do but yield to what they want and hope for the best.

By following this methodology to P.R.A.Y. for accessing capital, it significantly increases the likelihood of receiving the type of financing you need in the shortest possible time frame.

Learn more about topics discussed in this chapter from the workbook, my book *Get Your Business Financed Faster and Easier; The P.R.A.Y. System to Access Capital,* and courses available at the Small Business Pro University (www.SBProU.com).

Key Learnings

1) Your personal credit score and report are critical.
2) Having collateral is extremely helpful.
3) Your taxes must be filed and hopefully show that you are making money.
4) No surprises – full disclosure is a must. It's better to declare something negative than for it to become a surprise later in the process because credibility is one of the pillars for being able to obtain financing.

Chapter 5 – Is It Me or Are My Employees Crazy?

We've all heard the saying, "No man is an island" by John Donne. It's probably truer in business than most places in life. We can only work so many hours and produce so much on our own. As your business grows, you'll have to build capacity by hiring people and it's time to seek help once your revenues and working capital are consistently at a level that would support the cost of an employee. Adding people will inherently change your organization whether for the better or for the worse. As it is your organization, it is your job to effectively integrate everyone into the team so that they can make the maximum contribution to the business's success. Although it might sound simple, it is much easier said than done. Managing, hiring, and dealing with people is one of the most challenging responsibilities most entrepreneurs and business owners face. Michael Gerber, in the *eMyth Revisited,* says that you can't manage people, but you can manage systems. Gerber laid out the keys to building a successfully functioning team within your organization.

Systems & Processes

So, what does that mean? It means that you need to put in the work up front to create and formalize the structure and processes within your business. This is a key part of working **ON** your business. You need to implement standard processes for everything as well as the systems that they support.

"Your Primary Role Will Shift from Managing to Leading"

As your organization grows, your primary role will shift from managing your organization to leading it. This is best done by setting the example, by setting policies, and by developing the best culture (environment) to achieve your goals. All three of these tasks are things that you cannot delegate to someone else and are critical in moving your organization forward. Given that you've probably never done this before, you will most likely need outside help in terms of coaching, consulting and/or training. If you do this right, your role at the company will be more as a symbol, a communicator, and a facilitator, as opposed to focusing on the day to day business operations. Now, this is important for moving from working **IN** your business to working **ON** your business and must be completed if you ever want to be in a position to spend most of your time working **ON THE FUTURE** of your business.

Since most entrepreneurs and small business owners are usually in phase one, working on their business, they spend a lot of time working closely with employees without much separation. This results in developing personal relationships that can make it hard to effectively supervise your employees and manage your business. They experience emotional attachment, conflict, and a confusion of roles. As a supervisor, your job is to make sure that the work gets done and to ensure that your employees are doing their job. Many times, this type of relationship can be antagonistic (how many times have you hated your boss?). However, as a manager, your job is to be a leader, to empower people, and to inspire people to do their best. How can you do this effectively if they don't like you, respect you, and trust you? Usually, the supervisor is the one to be tough, to deliver bad news, and to provide feedback to employees about their performance. Conversely, as a manager, your job is to work on the business in terms of developing strategies and plans that consist of ways to increase sales and productivity. Given this inherent conflict that most small business owners have, it makes employee relationships especially difficult. You must deal with personal issues and multiple personalities, which can be draining. The bottom line - it is difficult, if not nearly impossible to be both a good supervisor and an effective manager at the same time. You are playing two different roles with conflicting demands making it difficult to do either one of them well and it becomes too much for one person to handle. The result is that entrepreneurs and small business owners experience stress and they sometimes try to avoid conflict with their staff members, rather than confronting and dealing with sensitive issues that require their attention.

One of my clients that has been in business for 20+ years has 12 employees and no real supervisor. As a result, he must supervise all of them, which is a full-time job. Couple that with his business being open 12 hours a day, 7 days per week, and he also works operations, doing customer service and helping to deliver the product. This makes it a job and a half. How can he find the time to work **ON** his business and get to Stage 2? The first step was reading the *eMyth Revisited*, helping him to understand what he needs to do and why. His next step was closing one day per week to rest and start working on the business. This is a good start, but without a supervisor he will never be able to move his business forward in any meaningful way.

This stressor can breed an owner's contempt for his or her employees. Small business owners really hate it when I tell them this, but it is their fault. Since they own the business, have control, and can make all the rules, they have the tools to create a better situation. The difficulty is that the business owner may not have learned important supervisory and management skills necessary to be more effective at their job. This point is brought home through my favorite lines from *Remember the Titans*, a movie I really like.

71

It comes when the team leader is chastising a player for not doing his best and not focusing on helping his teammates by saying that he had a bad attitude. The player turns around and mentions blatant issues he has with things that are happening unfairly and says, "Attitude reflects leadership." That was a turning point in the team's coming together because at that point the team leader actually realized that he wasn't doing his job. He started taking responsibility for everyone and everything that's happening with the team, creating an environment that inspired people to do their best. As a result, the team came together, started having fun, and played better than ever. This is an important lesson to learn because it is your job as the business owner.

So, what should you do? It is important to create a structure as such that includes a supervisor, so you'll be able to be an effective manager. This is the first step in building a sustainable organization. This entails allowing yourself to have some separation from your employees and having someone who is responsible for making sure that the operations run effectively. Make sure it is someone you can trust. Without that, it's almost impossible to be away from your business without worries, fear, and decreasing your revenues and profitability. Or losing money!

"Hire, Train, and Empower a Supervisor: Don't Micro-Manage"

Just having a supervisor is not enough. The supervisor needs to be trained and empowered so that he or she can do their job well. Training isn't that difficult, but the empowerment part is very challenging for entrepreneurs and business owners because they are so used to micromanaging. But creating the right structure and the right systems can provide the information business owners and managers need to know about what is happening without having to micro-manage. A manager's job is to work through the supervisors rather than directly with all the employees. That's extremely difficult when you've been working side by side with the employees and they are used to going to you directly. However, it is critical to support the chain of command so that the supervisors can supervise effectively. For example, in the military, you usually have a sergeant who takes orders from the officers, relaying them to the troops and ensuring that they are carried out. In those situations, the troops usually don't really like their sergeant (supervisor) at times, but the orders are carried out. The officers are above the fray since their role is to set an example, lead, and communicate. It is much easier for everyone to do their job effectively when you have the separation.

Managing employees is much more difficult without the right systems in place that help them to know your expectations and allow them to take initiative to do their jobs. As a result, employees can easily lose focus and not be as engaged when there is confusion about what they need to do. Creating the structure, processes, and systems for a business is not necessarily easy or quick. However, it is very logical and extremely effective.

First, you start by creating structure. Second, by formalizing processes. You should have specific processes and a system for delivering your products and services consistently. You also need to have a process for your record keeping, for your marketing and sales, for your operations, and for your administrative processes. For example, the marketing process could include how your employees answer the phone, the information they request, and how it is retained for use within the organization. Operational processes could include how you make or deliver your product or service, how it's distributed or provided to your customers, and how you keep track of your inventory. For service businesses, it would include your process for delivering the services that you offer, where they are provided to clients, and how the service offerings are developed. Don't forget your administrative processes, which includes how records are kept, the way new employees are on-boarded, and your regulatory compliance. Each business function has many different processes that are used to accomplish its objective. Systems are a combination of processes either within or among the different business functions that work together to accomplish the desired results and provide feedback and information that can be used to run the business more effectively.

For example, you may notice when you call certain organizations, whomever you get answers the phone the same way and asks similar questions. This is not by accident. It is a formalized procedure that was developed for the company's brand and sales process. I'm sure you've been to McDonald's and seen how quickly they can put your order together from start to finish. When you approach the register, they always welcome you in a similar way and all employees are wearing either blue or brown uniforms with the company insignia. They will always try to upsell - ask you if you want fries, a drink, or to super-size your order. Those are examples of McDonalds' sales and marketing processes. You will also notice that each time you order something, you get a consistent result. That's because there are specific operational processes that they have when producing your order. This goes down to even how many pickles you get and where they are placed on the burger. Examples of their administrative processes includes how the order is entered, providing a customer with a receipt, and retaining the register tape for analysis and management.

The first step is laying out an organizational chart that shows the various roles that you plan to have within the organization over the next few years. Then, it's important to indicate who is currently doing the work for each of these roles. The responsibility may be shared by multiple people, some employees will have multiple positions, and certain roles may have nobody doing them at this time. For this to work, there needs to be a plan for growing the organization, since growth brings opportunities, excitement, and employee buy-in. The next step is to develop a path for increased responsibility and growth within the organization, rather than just providing dead-end jobs.

Developing processes is formalizing and standardizing how things should be done in detail – definitely not rocket science. Systems must be created to help processes work together effectively and efficiently, based on feedback and information from various sources throughout the company. You must create an organizational structure before you can have processes, and you must have processes before you can develop systems.

According to Michael Gerber in the *E-myth Revisited*, if the business is to thrive, it must move beyond the founder: a business that is wholly dependent on the founder and his or her abilities is not really a business, but rather a very burdensome job for the founder. Every time they are out sick or take a vacation or are otherwise absent, their business stops too.

A stage three business is one where the founder has created a system so that the business can run itself without their constant presence. The book describes this as the "Franchise Prototype". It does not suggest that you necessarily try and create a business to be franchised, but rather just to treat it as if it were in some critical respects: you need a well-documented system to run the business. Instead of running the business (fixing bicycles, writing computer programs, cooking), you need to work on the business - you need to spend time creating a business that is an entity that can operate and thrive. When creating systems and processes the goals are to:

- Provide consistent value to your customers

- Not require brilliant people to work it
- Empower ordinary people to consistently do high quality work
- Document everything in operations manuals
- Be uniform for people across the organization

Learn more about topics discussed in this chapter from the workbook and courses available at the Small Business Pro University (www.SBProU.com).

<u>Key Learnings</u>

1) Adding people inherently changes your organization whether for the good or for the bad.
2) Managing, hiring, and dealing with people is one of the most challenging responsibilities of most small business owners.
3) It is difficult, if not nearly impossible to be both a good supervisor and an effective manager at the same time.
4) Since you own the business, have control, and can make all the rules, only you have the tools to create a better situation.
5) Creating the structure, processes, and systems for a business is not necessarily easy or quick.
6) You must create an organizational structure before having processes, and processes before developing systems.

Chapter 6 – Can I Get My Old Job Back?

Having a business is not for the faint of heart and there's a lot more to it than having a job. In a business, you're taking a lot of personal risk; you're the last one to get paid - that is, if there's any money left. Sometimes you even must go in your pocket and provide critically needed temporary funds, just to keep everything afloat. Often, it seems like the grass is greener on the other side. From time to time, you may lose more than a little sleep. So, why would you even want to have a business?

It takes a special breed of person to want to have and to operate a business. If you're one of them, you probably already know that many times they thrive on the challenge. However, no matter how good of a fit your temperament and personality are to become a business owner, there are always some dark days when you consider whether going the job route would have been better. Also, sometimes people come to the point where their business is simply no longer viable, and they need to find employment and regroup.

When first starting out in business, it can be especially challenging because there's so much work to do and never enough money - or time, for that matter. It often feels like you're working around the clock and possibly not even making any money. That can be both stressful and disheartening for many people. Often, entrepreneurs will give up on their dream - or think seriously about it. Truth time: even after your business is up and running, you're probably still going to be working harder than ever before and making less money than you expected. That can be a problematic situation as well. Especially when you can't afford to do things you used to do, and your personal expenses are not being met. Many entrepreneurs often think about quitting then. If you are an entrepreneur, and you've made it to this stage, there has been at least one moment in your experience that you considered throwing in the towel. Once you've tasted the forbidden fruit - experiencing the freedom, creativity, and control of having your own business, it's hard to give it up. That's why you find many entrepreneurs who end up selling their businesses and then starting new businesses, rather than returning to employment.

As your business grows and you start making some money, it can still be very stressful, due to cash flow issues or other challenges. One of the biggest challenges is not enjoying what you are doing since you must spend so much time working in your business. I run into many entrepreneurs who still consider going back and getting a job at different points during this stage.

For example, one of my clients, Briana Evans who owns Speech Quest, does speech therapy with a focus on children with autism. She has a passion for helping school-aged children through young adults. Her experience working in elementary schools in Brooklyn and Queens as well as high schools in the Bronx, kindled her desire to help children with speech or reading difficulties. Initially, she was working out of a back room within a Gymboree, along with one part-time employee. Her biggest challenges were getting enough clients to keep herself and her employee busy. At that time, she was working her behind off and only making a little bit of money. She thought about quitting at some point every day. We focused our sessions on developing her sales and marketing skills, developing her marketing strategy, and coming up with ideas based on what we discussed in Chapter 2. After a short time, her marketing efforts paid off and her number of clients increased significantly, to where she had to hire a second part-time therapist, and she was handling as many patients as possible. This led her to feel better about her situation and enjoy her business more, resulting in her only wanting to quit once every week or so. (A sign of improvement!)

This situation caused a new challenge because now Briana could barely handle all the customers she had, and that stress led her to no longer enjoy working with patients. And she once again thought about quitting daily. From there we focused our sessions on managing her growth as well as time management. Then, she found a new location where she would have her own space, a sublet, with more room and better access for herself and her clients. This really got her excited because she was able to create her very own environment for the business. It sparked her creativity by decorating it with her personal vision. It also gave her room to have two patient sessions at a time within the new space. Plus, she was able to set up her own office area and work space for managing the business. This once again changed her perspective and significantly reduced the frequency of how often she would think about quitting.

In the new space, Briana added another therapist and continued to market and grow her business. At this point, Briana was making more money, and everything seemed to be going really well. However, her marketing efforts continued to bring on new clients and she also brought on additional therapists as needed. This was both great and terrible. It was great because she was making more money and her business was doing well, but it was terrible because her business management responsibilities increased significantly, as well as the amount of paperwork to bill the insurance companies. This was compounded by the fact that she really didn't like doing administrative tasks or managing a lot of people. Eventually, she found a virtual assistant who took over scheduling and paperwork completion and submission, at a reasonable cost. This freed her up to focus on what she really liked to do. At this point, she started enjoying her business and only thought about quitting every month or so. (Still more improvement!)

"Thinking About Quitting is only Normal but Doing it is Rare. "

As her business continued to grow, an opportunity opened for her to take over the entire space that she was subletting. This gave her enough room to do sessions with an additional three clients, all at the same time. It also allowed her once again to be creative in designing her new space to make it into what she always envisioned. Plus, she was able to hire additional people and set her schedule the way she wanted. Her biggest challenge was being able to hand off new clients to her other therapists because people knew and wanted her to work personally with their children. Her business continued to expand, and she was able to figure out different ways to overcome this challenge, but she was really enjoying her business during this period and rarely thought about quitting. Of course, nothing lasts forever, so other challenges arose which impacted how she thought about the business and made her think about quitting more often. As you can see, entrepreneurs go through many different stages and phases with their businesses because there are always new challenges to overcome. Facing these challenges can impact how you think about possibly going back to the simple life of just having a job. However, if you are a true entrepreneur, going back and taking a regular 9 to 5 becomes almost impossible ... even though sometimes it seems like it would be better. When I was in the Navy, they would say that a complaining sailor is a happy sailor, which I think is true for entrepreneurs as well. So, thinking about quitting is only normal, but actually doing it is rare.

Think about why you went in to business to begin with. People leave people, rather than companies. (Remember your old boss?) That may be why you made the change as well. When people start businesses, many times they do not realize the level of risk they are taking and the amount of commitment they must have. When you have a business, it's not as easy as just up and quitting or giving notice because your business life is intertwined with your personal life. Having a business is like going into war. And to be successful in war, you must always press forward, despite any challenges that you face. It's best to think of it as going to the shore of your enemy and burning your ships. There is no looking back, the only way home is to fight through every challenge to survive. Having a business is also like raising a child. It will take center stage in your life and become part of your identity. Although some people think that they can make other things a priority, that is extremely difficult while building a business until you get to Phase 3, when everything is running smoothly and you're working **ON THE FUTURE** of your business. Not only is having a business a personal commitment, it is also a financial commitment - and your personal and your business financial pictures are intertwined. It is not as easy as up and quitting or giving notice. This can make it even more difficult to sell or leave your business.

For example, one of my clients felt like his business became overwhelming because his sales were declining, his partner was not helping as much as expected, and he wanted to make his children more of a priority, plus he was making less than half as much money as he was previously. Unfortunately, he had financed the business and had family members as guarantors on the loan. Even worse, the business had declined to the point where the current value was less than the amount owed on it. Also, the owner was still in Stage 1, working **IN** the business so without them there was really no business. As their coach, I had to deliver them the bad news that it wasn't possible to sell at this time and closing at this time would ruin both their personal financial position and those of the family members who signed on just to help them out and were not really involved in the business. I let him know that the only way out was to work even harder on the business to increase its revenue and profitability enough to create value to where it could be sold for enough to cover the loan. However, once you turn the business around, you probably won't want to sell any more because everything will be in a much better place. But that was the only way out without significantly damaging the lives of his immediate family and his extended family. That was a hard pill to swallow and took a couple of weeks before he fully embraced his situation.

Sometimes it does make sense to recommend that someone discontinue their business or switch to part-time status and find outside employment. Why might that be the case? Number one, their business model might not be viable, and they need to make some money to position themselves to try again at another time. Number two, their personal situation may have changed so that they no longer have the time or the focus to do it right or there is a financial need that the business cannot help them with at the current time. I also encourage people who really aren't up to the challenge at this time to consider whether they should or should not move forward with their business. However, the most difficult situation is when I'm working with someone who is in business and really loves it, but they are undercapitalized, and their financial/credit position will not allow them to get to the level that needs to be achieved for the business to be sustainable. Therefore, they must earn some money part-time or full-time to keep it going. They may have to scale back what they are doing with their business to earn some money.

On the flip side, I coach a lot of people who are either seeking to start a business or currently have a part-time business and want to make it full-time. I especially like working with them because they have time to plan and position things without the stress of their business needing to make money immediately. I can have the greatest impact because I can work with them on their business plan and strategy to ensure that their business model is viable before they take the plunge. Second, we can figure out their startup costs and fixed expenses in advance to make sure that they start out with enough capital to implement their plan and be successful. This is key, especially because most small businesses start out under-funded which is very difficult, if not impossible to overcome successfully. By having a good plan and enough capital to implement it, you significantly increase your potential for success and increase the amount of success that you ultimately will achieve. Most of the time it makes more sense for them to keep working at a job and saving more of their own money, working on their business part-time while developing their business plan. It's always best to already have clients and revenue before you go into business full-time. Otherwise, it may take several months, if not longer, before your business is making enough money to cover your personal expenses. It is also better to use as much of your own money as possible because it takes time to obtain outside money, and there's a cost to obtaining funds from other sources. Plus, you won't have to make loan payments, which reduces your cash flow and makes your situation riskier. However, sometimes you "gotta do what you gotta do."

For example, I coached Kimberly Sumpter, owner of Wax Kandy Candles. She specializes in the production of scented and customized keepsake candles. As the head candle maker, her goal is to produce candles that are highly fragrant and beautifully crafted by giving special attention to details and customer requests. They pour each candle by hand using premium quality wax, essential oils, and fragrances.

Kimberly was working at another job full-time and her part-time business was thriving. When I met her, she was interested in transitioning to her business full-time. We talked about and wrote down the pluses and minuses of each scenario. I had her put together an Excel model to compare the financial impact of each option that included startup costs, projected fixed costs, and personal expenses. When Kimberly determined how much her business would have to generate to replace what she was currently earning, she realized that it would take quite a while. That did not even include accounting for her health benefits. Not surprisingly, Kimberly decided to continue working at her job to maintain her personal financial situation and save additional money for when she is ready to run her business full-time. She also hired a part-time employee who helped her to continue growing her business, while maintaining her full-time job. As a result, she will have more savings, fewer personal expenses, and higher revenues from her business whenever she decides to go at it full time.

Learn more about topics discussed in this chapter from the workbook and courses available at the Small Business Pro University (www.SBProU.com).

Key Learnings

1) In a business, you're taking a lot of personal risk; you're the last one to get paid - that is, if there's any money left.
2) As a business owner you will most likely be working harder than ever before and making less money than you expected.
3) It is not as easy as just up and quitting or giving notice because your business life is intertwined with your personal life both socially and financially.

4) Having a business is like raising a child. It will take center stage in your life and become part of your identity.

Chapter 7 – How Will I Ever Retire?

"How Will I Ever Retire?"

As the great Steven Covey, author of the book entitled *The Seven Habits of Highly Effective People* said, "Whatever you do, it is important to begin with the end in mind. Whenever starting a business, you should already be thinking about your exit strategy." Or, in the words of Michael Gerber, author of the *eMyth*, "An entrepreneur's job is to figure out how he is going to get ***out*** of his or her business." Of course, that's what you should do, but few small business owners start out that way because they have limited vision. Their retirement plans usually aren't thought about until it's almost too late. While it's also true of the general population, it's even truer for the entrepreneur. As a business owner, you are 100% responsible for figuring out and implementing a retirement strategy. Good strategies need a lot of time to implement successfully, so it's important to start early. Most entrepreneurs that I work with don't really start thinking about this until they're at least 50 years of age, which is very late. Plus, many of them are under the misconception that their business can actually be sold for a lot of money. We'll get more into that a little bit later, but first let's talk about what sort of things can be done to prepare for retirement effectively.

"Get a permanent life insurance policy as early as possible"

First and foremost, you need to get a permanent life insurance policy as early in life as possible. Permanent life insurance such as whole life, universal life, or variable life builds cash value and provides a permanent death benefit for your family. On the other hand, term life insurance does not build cash value and expires, requiring you to buy additional insurance at a much higher price when you are older. The trade-off is that whole life insurance premiums cost generally twice as much as term life premiums for a given age. However, cash value life insurance is usually a much better choice unless you're 50 years old or more. This is also an investment for your business because lenders usually require you to have enough life insurance to cover the loan as a condition of providing financing. The proceeds you earn from life insurance are not taxed, so keep that in mind as well when you are deciding how much to purchase.

Second, I shouldn't even have to tell you this, but you need to be making personal Social Security tax payments to ensure you are able to take advantage of this benefit. To do this, you must either pay yourself as an employee and/or show a profit from your business in most years. Paying into Social Security will also help you to insure against long term disability. In addition, it will also provide a survivors' benefit for your dependents.

Third, you should set up some type of qualified retirement plan, so you can put away money for retirement on a tax deferred basis. This can take the form of a 401K or a profit-sharing plan within your business and a traditional IRA or an annuity on a personal basis.

You should have disability insurance. Most entrepreneurs don't really think about the risk and the consequences of becoming disabled, even though it is a somewhat common occurrence. Without insurance, you may not have the income to sustain yourself and your business, should you become disabled, which could result in the loss of your biggest asset.

An extremely important factor, which you may not have control over, is staying married. As you know, divorce can be very taxing from a personal, professional, emotional, and financial perspective.

Rosanne DeTorres, Esq., of the firm DeTorres & DeGeorge, advises the following to business owners facing a potential divorce:

"Protect your interest with a pre-marital agreement. Spell out your pre-existing business assets and have your spouse waive any claim to your business in the future. Assess and document the level of your spouse's involvement in your business. A spouse that lacks involvement in the business has a reduced claim to the business value."

She also recommends the following:

- Review your options for establishing a buy-sell agreement, corporation, LLC, or a living trust to restrict ownership and ownership transfer. Revise your partnership agreement to require that the other partners have the option to buy out the interests of the divorcing partner and his or her spouse.
- Carefully establish, fund, and manage your business with separate assets. Avoid co-mingling business assets with personal assets and business accounts with personal accounts. Pay yourself a market-rate salary.
- If a business is at issue in the divorce, a value must be placed on it. Agree on a number you both can live with. Then consider how to distribute it to your spouse - by cash payment, by an offset against other assets you will waive, or with installment payments."

Not only does the financial settlement impact your retirement, but your business won't make as much money for a while, since you won't be able to focus on it in the same way. Even worse, divorce could result in having to sell your business or losing ownership to your spouse, which puts a dent in your earnings potential. The lyrics of the old Johnnie Taylor song say it all, "It's cheaper to Keep Her," (or him).

Last, but definitely not least, is maximizing the value of your business and developing a viable exit strategy or strategies. Your exit strategy could be any of the following, individually or in combination:

- Selling the business: to a partner, to a competitor, to an investor
- Taking it public
- Developing your business to a point where it can function well totally independently of you
- Transitioning your business to the next generation
- Merger or acquisition
- Transferring your business to employee ownership
- Franchising or licensing your business

A financial advisor once asked me to value the business of a 65 year old doctor he was working with on retirement planning. The doctor was looking to sell his business quickly and retire early due to age and health issues. He had little savings and not much equity in his home, so he was expecting the proceeds of the sale to sustain him. Although he expected close to $1 million, my valuation was less than $100k. Why is that? Since he's the only doctor, the only things of value were the customer list, used equipment, and a lease. Without him the business had minimal value. Eventually he was able to sell for a little over $100k, but he had to stay on and work part-time for 3 years. Definitely, not the retirement he planned.

"A Strong, Recognizable Brand Drives Repeat Business"

Regardless of your exit strategy, your goal needs to be to maximize the value of your business. Many times, entrepreneurs and small business owners significantly overestimate the value of their business. This could be for many reasons. Here's how to avoid them: separate yourself from emotional attachment to the business, understand how business valuation works, develop relationships with potential buyers over time, set up the business so it can run without you, show income or profitability, grow and/or be able to scale up, purchase hard assets like real estate, and develop a strong, recognizable brand that drives repeat business.

Focusing on these items is really what running your business like a pro is all about. Our methodologies are focused on helping entrepreneurs and small business owners maximize the value of their businesses through running the most successful business possible. It all starts with an accurate external assessment and valuation scoring, so that you can objectively understand where you are. From there, you must have a clear vision of what you are trying to achieve. The more detailed, the better. Once you have these, you have the input necessary to develop an optimum path to achieve your vision. The exit should be a part of that vision. Do research and perform analysis to come up with recommendations for the best path to achieve your goals. Having a strategy and a plan is only helpful if you put them into action. While implementing the plan, you will learn a lot and these learnings can be utilized to improve upon your strategy and planning. This is a planning process that needs to be done on an annual basis. Have a feedback loop to make the necessary adjustments based on your business's actual experience. By doing this, you will be running your business like a pro.

It is essential to surround yourself with a professional team of advisors, including a seasoned business coach, an accountant, an attorney, a financial advisor, etc. Maintaining good business and personal credit will have a huge impact on the value of your business, as well.

Similar to real estate, there really are only three ways to value a business:

1. Whatever someone is willing to pay.
2. Value it relative to a similar business.
3. Through fundamental analysis, using the discounted cash flow methodology, which is projecting future cash flow for the business and discounting them back to the present at an appropriate rate relative to the risk. Projecting future cash flow can be difficult because nobody really knows the future. However, forecasts can be made based on all available information.

One problem is that people will come up with different forecasts and valuations based on the same information. The second piece is figuring out the correct rate to use for discounting those cash flows back to the present value. Financial risk is based on the variability of return, so that a business with cash flow that fluctuates in a wide range is riskier than a similar business that fluctuates in a narrow range. Investors require a higher rate of return on an investment that is riskier. A higher required rate of return decreases the present value through the discounting process. That's why you only get a 1% return on your bank account, because there is zero risk of you not getting your money back. Discounting a cash flow is the opposite of appreciation or earning interest on an investment. For example, if the bank loans you $100 at a 10% interest rate, they are going to want $110 at the end of the year. That's appreciation. However, discounting is how much an investor is willing to give you today for a payment of $110 at the end of the year. If their required rate of return is 10%, they would be willing to loan you $100. However, if they view you as riskier, they might require a 15% rate of return. This would result in a present value of around $95 taking into account the additional return required to loan you the money. Investors demand an even higher rate of return for stocks because they are riskier. Equity valuation is more of an art than a science because it combines both qualitative and quantitative analysis. Keeping it really simple, small business values generally are between 2 and 4 times profits plus marketable assets minus liabilities. Generally, you don't need to spend money on a professional valuation unless it is required by a lender or an investor.

Not long ago I came across the Value Builder System, which is a statistically proven system for increasing the value of your company. At first, I was skeptical, but the more I learned, the better I liked it. So much so, that I recently became a Value Builder Adviser. It starts with a questionnaire which is used to determine your Value Builder Score out of 100. Companies with a score of 80+ generally get offers that are 71% higher than average scoring businesses.

The Value Builder System was designed by John Warrillow, author of the international bestseller *Built to Sell: Creating A Business That Can Thrive Without You.* I highly recommend you check it out to learn more about how to maximize the value of your business. The System focuses on helping you to concentrate on improving your score in each of the 8 key value drivers for businesses.

Learn more about topics discussed in this chapter from the workbook, my book *Exit Your Business More Profitably; The Keys to Effective Succession Planning,* and courses available at the Small Business Pro University (www.SBProU.com).

Key Learnings

1) An entrepreneur's job is to figure out how he or she is going to get ***out*** of his or her business.

2) As a business owner, you are 100% responsible for figuring out and implementing a retirement strategy.

3) Prepare for retirement early by purchasing permanent life insurance, paying social security taxes, setting up a retirement plan, obtaining disability insurance, and staying married.

4) Focus on maximizing the value of your business and developing a viable exit strategy or strategies. Start at least 5 years before you might want to sell.

5) Profits, not sales, drive the value of your company. A range of 2 – 4 times profits plus assets minus liabilities provides a general indication of value.

6) Obtain a Value Builder Score to see how your company rates in each of the 8 key business drivers. Visit www.SBProValueBuilder.com.

Section II – This Is How You Do It!

Chapter 8 – Running Your Business Like A Pro

In small business, there is a critical path that must be followed to become successful. It has worked for businesses in all types of industries and of all different sizes. It's a windy path that takes you from working **IN** your business to working **ON** your business to working **ON THE FUTURE** of your business.

SBPro Critical Path

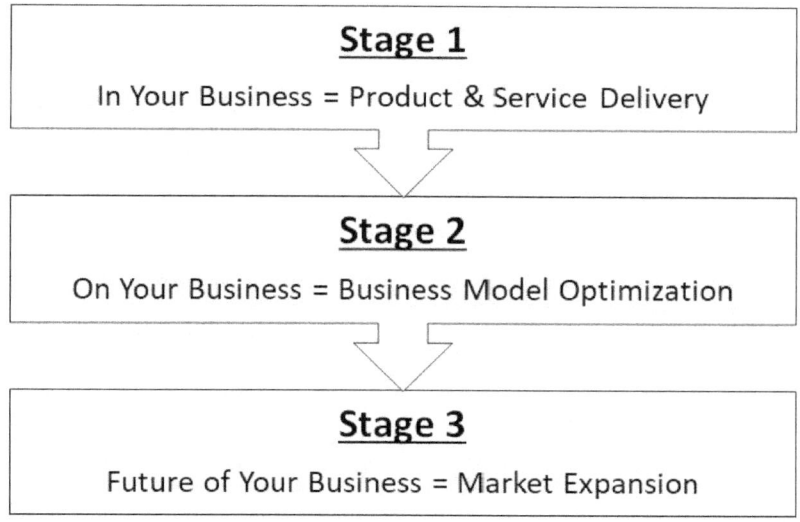

Stage 1
In Your Business = Product & Service Delivery

Stage 2
On Your Business = Business Model Optimization

Stage 3
Future of Your Business = Market Expansion

Now, everybody's heard about needing to work **ON** your business rather than **IN** your business, but unfortunately, most small business owners never make it to a point where they are actually working on their business. It's not necessarily due to a lack of desire, but a lack of direction, knowledge, and support - plus a lack of focus and a lack of necessary resources. One big problem is that there has not really been a clear understanding of the specific criteria and milestones involved in moving from stage to stage.

Working **ON THE FUTURE** of your business is a newer concept that we introduce as a third stage when your company is prepared for explosive growth. As an entrepreneur, it can be challenging because different skills and abilities are needed to make this transition from stage to stage, so it cannot be accomplished without a tremendous amount of learning, experimentation, training, and external resources, such as consultants. So, if you're going to run your business like a pro, you must be prepared to change both yourself and your organization and it's totally fine, and sometimes better to bring in professional management to run the company, rather than the business owner him or herself. One classic example of this is Apple® Computer and Steve Jobs, who was fired from his company because he was not prepared and able to change in the way the company needed at that time. However, he was able to come back and make significant contributions. Think about it - Apple might not be the Apple we know today had that not happened.

As outlined in the Preface, the key to running a successful business is making good business decisions. The ability to make good business decisions comes from gaining experience, proper planning, and getting good qualified counsel, plus increasing your knowledge about business in general. The previous chapters focused on learning from experience, helping you understand key challenges that businesses have, and offering you counsel as though you were one of my coaching clients. However, the most important thing you can do to assure your long term success is to put together a comprehensive planning process that incorporates the knowledge you have gained from your own experience, education, and expertise.

So, let's drill down a bit. What does it really mean to plan? People look at it in different ways, but for small business purposes, it's important to focus on a well-defined process with a few key steps. My Small Business Pro (SBPro) methodology is a three-step process that helps you to put together actionable plans to move your business forward. This process will meet you wherever you are in developing your enterprise and outline the next steps toward achieving your goal. It is a holistic process, in that it incorporates all facets of your business, i.e., your marketing/sales, your operations, your administration, and it considers how changes in one area of the business may affect other areas. For example, if you increase your marketing investment by $5,000, ask yourself these questions:

- How much do you need to increase sales for that to be a good investment of your limited funds?
- How much in additional sales and how many additional customers do you expect this investment to produce?
- Is this enough to make it worthwhile?
- Is this marketing consistent with your overall marketing strategy, and how will it contribute to the future value of the company?

If you take that a step further, when this marketing effort increases interest in your product, will you have enough inventory to satisfy the demand? Wouldn't it be nice to know these things before you make your marketing investment? Then you would have the information you need to make the right decision regarding that potential investment.

One key feature to keep in mind is that this is not a one-size fits all, but rather a custom plan that is specifically tailored to where your business currently stands. It focuses on developing a path to achieve your goals. In this vein, it allows you to continually make improvements, as opposed to trying to achieve perfection right out of the box. However, you do need to assure that you do everything with a certain level of quality.

You can utilize The Small Business Pro methodology to increase your likelihood of success and improve the level of success that you already have, based on the following three concepts:

1. <u>Assessment & Visualization</u> - Step 1 is an objective determination of where things currently stand and the development of a clear picture of where you are headed. Generally, you'll need an external, independent party to effectively assess the status of your business. You will also need information templates like those you will learn about in the next chapter. Those are for marketing and branding, sales, financial performance, and operational effectiveness and efficiency.

2. <u>Analysis & Recommendations</u> - Step 2 involves taking the information you have and doing additional research to formulate strategies to achieve your goals. You will do this by researching your competitors; learning who they are, what type, and how they compete with you; how you should position yourself based on your unique value proposition; discovering who your own industry's main players are, how fragmented it is, assessing its status - whether it's in a period of growth versus decline, comparative measures, technological changes; you will examine your target market in detail; it's size, profile, best ways to reach your prospects; viewing economic trends; get a handle on the expected rate of growth and decline, focusing on local trends, interest rates, real estate costs; learning as much as you can about best practices; proven strategies, proven systems, and processes and tactics; and seeking out potential

business partners, see who you can create alliances with to expand marketing, collaboration opportunities, provide a more complete solution for clients, as well as provide you with useful products and services, as well as education/expertise.

3. Implementation & Evaluation - Step 3 of your plan involves putting your plans into action to achieve the results you desire and adjust based on your findings. This includes determining metrics and key drivers that are measured regularly.

The SBPro methodology is consistent with the Frazier Formula for Success in my brother Evan Frazier's book entitled *Most Likely to Succeed*. The formula is: Vision times Plan times Attitude to the (R) power [Right attitude] = Success.

$$S = V \times P \times A^{(r)}$$

Each of these components is important because having a zero in any category results in zero success (anything multiplied by zero is zero). It also shows that your attitude is the most impactful driver of success. See how this aligns with the SBPro methodology: His vision is the SBPro assessment and envisioning phase; our analysis and recommendations phase is like his plan; and effective implementation and evaluation corresponds to the right attitude in his formula.

Everything starts with the Small Business Pro Assessment which outlines each of the 8 Success Drivers that must be developed through three stages to Run Your Business Like A Pro.

SBPro Methodology

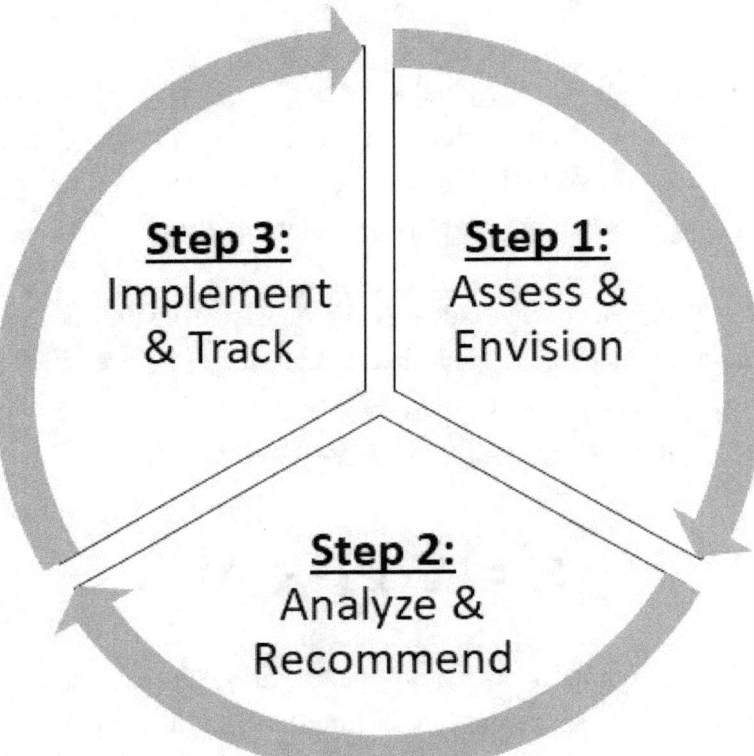

The Success Drivers measure where a small business stands in terms of each of the following categories:

SBPro® Assessment Form

Category	Area of Focus	Stage
Products and Services		
Customers		
Marketing		
Staffing		
Business Structure		
Financial Management		
Time Management		
Free Time		
SBPro® Score	**Average**	

Each Success Driver is measured to determine which stage the company is in. As a result, a small business can exist in different stages at the same time. The Small Business Pro (SBPro) Assessment measures the company's current stage in each category. The SBPro Methodology is focused on developing and implementing plans for transitioning to the next level in each category until all of them are in Stage 3.

For continuity, I refer to the same two business owner examples throughout Section II of the book: Iron Strong Jewelry owned by

Tina Tang, whom you met back in Chapter 2 and Exothermic owned by Paul Steck whom you will learn more about in Chapter 9. They are perfect businesses to compare because…

- Iron Strong Jewelry is a service business and Exothermic is a manufacturer
- Exothermic has employees and Iron Strong Jewelry doesn't
- Exothermic is B2B and Iron Strong Jewelry is B2C
- Iron Strong Jewelry is woman owned and Exothermic is not
- Exothermic revenues are greater than $1 million and Iron Strong Jewelry revenues are not
- Exothermic has been in business for 30+ years and Iron Strong Jewelry for fewer than five

I want you to think about how these businesses may be similar to or different from yours. Consider how their marketing/sales, operations and administrative needs compare. Also, try and use the 3 - step SBPro Methodology for your own business to see what you learn.

Learn more about topics discussed in this chapter from courses available at the Small Business Pro University (www.SBProU.com).

Key Learnings

1) Every business needs to have a defined process to move it forward.
2) The critical path for a successful entrepreneurial journey: working **IN** your business, then working **ON** your business, and finally working **ON THE FUTURE** of your business.

3) Most small business owners never even make it to working ON their business because they don't understand how or why.

4) You need to assess the current state of your business, analyze its needs for future growth, and develop and implement a growth plan using the SBPro Methodology.

5) SBPro Methodology Steps: Assessment and Envisioning, Analysis and Recommendations, Implementation and Tracking.

6) Give strong consideration to hiring outside consultants to help you through this process.

Chapter 9 – Step 1: Assessment & Envisioning

According to author and productivity expert Steven Covey, it's important to begin with the end in mind. That is also a critical element of being able to run your business like a pro. It's impossible to develop a good plan to achieve anything if you don't know where you are going. However, it is equally important to know where you are starting from. "TEMET NOSCE" for all you Matrix fans, which means "know thyself" in Latin. It's critical to do a thorough assessment, and many times you'll need an outside perspective to provide a more accurate picture of your current state. This is because business owners are too close to their own companies to really "see the forest through the trees", as the expression goes. Once you know where you are, it's important to know where you want to go. If you don't have a destination, any road will get you there. Creating a vision that is as detailed as possible will allow you to have a clear picture of what you desire to achieve and make it much more likely that you will in fact reach the level of success that you desire.

Step 1:
SBPro® Assessment & Envisioning

Where You Are?

Where You Are Going?

Assessment

Knowing that you need to do an assessment and knowing how to do one are two different things. There are many different levels and types of assessments that can be done. However, to run your business like a pro, you'll need to start with the SBPro Assessment to determine what stage your business is in across a variety of categories. Figuring this out will provide an understanding of the things that you are doing well and the areas you need to work on. It also provides a path for you to follow.

When completing the SBPro Assessment, you should break it down into what you are currently doing successfully, which things you are working on, and which things you haven't really started. From there, you'll know what specific areas to target. Targeting these areas will require further, more detailed analysis of additional information about your business.

Iron Strong Jewelry, owned by Tina Tang, produces jewelry developed for women to celebrate physical fitness achievements. She also does physical training but did not really highlight that or focus on that activity from a business perspective. While assessing her current situation, we learned that she has no employees and that most of her revenues come from online sales, but she wasn't sure how they originated. Tina spent a lot of time developing new products that were of a very high quality, but more expensive than the competition. She has very limited funds to invest in the business and is seeking to significantly increase her revenues. Although Tina had a website with e-commerce capabilities, it needed an upgrade to make it more user friendly in order to simplify the buying process. She was using paid advertisements to attract customers but didn't really know the impact of the ads. Plus, she had a very wide target market and was not targeting the right people, which made it impossible to effectively reach viable prospects given her limited budget. A valuable but underutilized asset is her company name, Iron Strong, and the ability to use it for marketing and branding purposes. My assessment of Tina's business status was the following:

Category	Area of Focus	Stage
Products and Services	Optimization	2
Customers	Repeat Biz & Referrals	2
Marketing	Finding Target Market	1
Staffing	Self	1
Business Structure	Informal and Flexible	1
Financial Management	Taxes and Compliance	1
Time Management	Operations	1
Free Time	Some	2
SBPro Score	**Average**	**1.375**

I also had an opportunity to work with Paul Steck, President of Exothermic in Kenilworth, New Jersey. Since 1972, his company has been a pioneer in the RIM (Reaction Injection Molding) industry. Paul purchased the business 15 years ago. The company creates molded plastic parts through a process that allows them to create fast, low-cost, high tolerance, precision molds. RIM is a superior process for creating large, complex parts and the company's personnel are experts at finishing (sanding, painting, and assembly) them. The company also has a core competency in working with product designers to develop and create the optimal molds used in forming their parts. There are not many companies that use this process, which is the most cost-effective way to create small and medium size quantities of plastic parts. Paul's primary customers are medical device manufacturers that have him produce components for their products as well as those in electronics and lab instruments. Generally, his product batches can run from one to one hundred parts at a time, but he gets a lot of repeat business and longer-term contracts. In addition, the company has procured an exclusive right to manufacture and distribute a newly developed plastic material that is lighter and stronger than most metals. This presents a huge opportunity for the company, provided they are prepared and able to take advantage of it.

He brought me on through an organization known as New Jersey Manufacturing Experience Program (NJMEP) as an outsourced CFO to help him with succession planning. Paul was also very involved in all areas of the business and did most of the quotes for new business. His goal was to position himself to either sell, transition, or just be the owner without having to work in his business within the next 5 years. He also wanted to establish new Key Performance Indicators (KPI's) to more effectively track progress and improve performance. His vision was to have the company running smoothly without him needing to be there. We worked to assess his current situation to determine the optimal path for him to implement and achieve this goal.

Initially, we looked at his current challenge to identify his immediate needs. The company was way behind on delivering customer orders and their on-time percentage was declining. At that time, there was a significant backlog of orders that needed to be produced and shipped. To make things even more challenging, he lost his production manager, who had overseen the manufacturing process. In addition, he had staffing challenges in recruitment and retention, making it difficult to increase their output and catch up on the backlog. Fortunately, Paul had good, long term relationships with most clients, which helped limit the negative impact of the order backlogs. This allowed him to work with his clients to adjust delivery dates in many cases since his products are not commodities, making it difficult for customers to leave. Paul also owned his facility and had many long-term employees that were committed to the business. My assessment of Paul's Business was the following:

Category	Area of Focus	Stage
Products and Services	Line Extension & New Markets	3
Customers	Repeat Business and Referrals	2
Marketing	Exploiting Target Market	2
Staffing	Leading Management	3
Business Structure	Developing Processes	2
Financial Management	Financial Statements & Analysis	2
Time Management	Operations	1
Free Time	Some	2
SBPro Score	**Average**	**2.125**

Envisioning

In the Bible it says, "Without a vision, the people will perish." This is also true in terms of small business because without a vision your business will perish. Even though this step is crucial, many small businesses owners have never really gotten to it or done it well. Part of the reason is that they don't really know what it means or how to do it. So, we've created a basic template for starting. This template breaks down some of the key things you should plan to achieve in your business. To do it most effectively, it helps to have a short-term (one year), medium-term (three years), and long-term (five years) vision for what you want to achieve. When you are putting together your vision, there are some important components you want to quantify. The first thing you want to look at are the number of locations you see yourself having in each of these time frames, whether it be physical and/or virtual platforms. You also need to have an idea of how much revenue and profit that you expect to reach in each time frame. In addition, it's important to think about what your organizational structure will be and how many employees you plan to have. You should also think about how you expect your products and services mix to evolve. A few operational measures you should include in the vision are as follows: how many customers you will have, the average amount of each sale you will be making, what percentage of your business you want your largest customer to represent, and how much financing you expect to need and when.

"You Must See It Before You Can Do It"

By clarifying your short-term, medium-term, and long-term expectations in terms of these categories, it becomes much easier to analyze what it would take to achieve your goals. For example, by knowing your current sales and the sales you envision having in the future, you can determine how much you to need to grow each year. Then you can take that information to develop a strategy to accomplish your goal. However, without a clear vision, you don't have the necessary information to come up with a good plan.

What does it mean to envision? It's defined as being able to see the future today, what your business will look like in the future. We're not talking here about a vision *statement*. Instead, we're focused on envisioning the future state of the business. This picture must demonstrate the level of success that you seek and motivate you to want to achieve it. It must be your personal vision and you must own it. Like anything else, your vision needs to be flexible, but not so flexible that it would change on a whim. Rather, each year it is good to re-evaluate your vision as part of the planning process to incorporate the experiences you've had and what you've learned. Based on your actual sales in the coming year versus the plan, you may want to expand or increase your vision, or cut back your vision in terms of future revenues. You may also have changes in the marketplace that necessitate a change of strategy and a new vision for where you want the company to go. Having clear quantitative measures as part of your vision is very important. However, you shouldn't get caught up in analysis-paralysis and sacrifice the good to try and achieve perfection. It's only a guide and the direction is more important than the magnitude. However, not having a vision provides no information to work with and doesn't allow you to plan effectively.

For example, IBM has gone through many shifts in its vision for the future over the years. Initially, they started out as International Business Machines, where they manufactured and sold different office equipment for businesses. From there, that evolved into developing early computer systems for business application.

These computers were huge and would fill up entire rooms. As technology advanced and components became smaller and less expensive, their vision shifted to personal computers, where they ended up being the market leader. As things changed, and computers became more of a commodity, IBM envisioned itself as more of a service provider, bringing in technology and information solutions to organizations rather than manufacturing and selling hardware. These shifts in vision, based on their capabilities, learning, and the marketplace, allowed IBM to remain relevant and continue growing, as opposed to other large companies with a more limited and stagnant vision, such as Blockbuster, Kodak, and JC Penney's.

Tina Tang's original vision was to target women for jewelry focused on fitness and grow her revenues (Stage 2). Through our envisioning process, we talked about creating quantitative goals for how many employees she plans to have, how much revenue she would like to achieve, and how she can evolve and strengthen her brand. In addition, we talked about some new products and the potential for combining her fitness and jewelry businesses under the Iron Strong Brand. We cross marketed the two businesses and created awareness with her training clients that she does jewelry, and with her jewelry clients that she does training. It strengthened her story of why she did jewelry celebrating women's fitness. By co-marketing, she unexpectedly grew her fitness business more than her jewelry business.

Paul's vision was to develop his business to a point where he would focus on new opportunities for growing the business and had maximum flexibility to spend more time traveling, while knowing that the business was running well without him being there (Stage 3). He sees the company introducing a new type of material and mold making process that would revolutionize the industry and result in significant growth for the company. He also envisions greater automation of production and information management to improve productivity and increase capacity.

We learned a lot about ourselves and our goals by completing Step 1 (Assessment and Envisioning) of the SBPro Methodology. Now we are ready to move on to Chapter 10 where we will use what we learned to complete Step 2 (Analysis and Recommendations).

Learn more about topics discussed in this chapter from courses available at the Small Business Pro University (www.SBProU.com).

Key Learnings

1) It is very difficult to assess yourself accurately - get help.
2) The SBPro Assessment is a powerful tool that is easy to use.
3) Envisioning your business - you must see it before you can do it.

Chapter 10 – Step 2: Analysis & Recommendations

By now, you have a pretty good idea that your success in business will not be by accident, but rather by design. By following each of the steps in the SBPro Methodology, your business will achieve measurable growth and progress. In Step 2, analysis involves taking the assessment information as well as detailing where you currently are and combining it with where you envision yourself being in the future (which we gathered in the previous Chapter 9) to determine the best course of action to achieve your goals. Analysis is going to combine that information along with additional research, both qualitative and quantitative, to develop a forecast of what you expect to happen under different scenarios. From there, you will seek to recommend the optimal plan for achieving your goals. Analysis and recommendations for each business are different, depending on the type of company and its current stage.

Step 2:
SBPro® Analysis & Recommendations

Develop Strategy

Business Plans

Analysis

It's critical to perform financial analysis using the SBPro Business Model formula and optimization strategies you learned about in Chapter 3. Start by pulling the following information from your financial statements from the most recent year: Sales (Revenue), Variable Expenses (COGs = Cost of Goods Sold), Gross Profit, Fixed (Operating) Expenses, and Operating Profit. If you have been in business for less than 1 year or are just starting out, these items must be estimated for year one.

SBPro® Business Model (i.e. Income Statement or P&L)		
Revenue	+	
Variable Expenses (COGS)	-	
Gross Profit	=	
Fixed Expenses	-	
Profit	=	

With this information, you can begin to optimize the business model to develop a realistic plan to achieve your revenue and profitability goals. This is an iterative process, such that it requires repetition in order to make improvements and determine the best solution. This is best done in a spreadsheet to develop financial projections for the next 3 years and easily update the entire model with each adjustment.

Here is an example of how you should approach putting together an initial SBPro Business Model analysis and 3 year projection. The process starts with actual Income Statement (P&L) information and assumes the envisioning process goal is to grow Revenue from $100k to $175k and maximize Profit over the next 3 years. This requires an annual Revenue growth rate of 21%. Therefore, year 1 revenue is calculated to be $120k, year 2 is $145k, and year 3 is $175k.

Then we calculate the Variable Cost (COGS) Factor (VCF = COGS / Revenue = $28k / $100k = 28%) from actual P&L information. This means that it costs 28 cents out of every dollar in revenue to provide your product(s) and/cr service(s) to a customer. COGS has a direct relationship with sales (COGS = COGS Factor * Sales). This relationship is very important because it makes calculating breakeven sales possible. Therefore, COGS for year 1 is $33.6k, year 2 is $40.6k, and year 3 $49k.

Gross Profit (GP) is the just difference between Revenue and COGS (GP = Revenue – COGS) and Fixed (Operating) Expenses are also obtained from actual P&L information. Initially we assume that fixed (operating) expenses remain constant at $41.5k for each of the 3 years. Finally, Operating Profit is the difference between Gross Profit and Operating Expenses (Operating Profit = GP – Operating Expenses).

Revenue needed to achieve both sales goals and breakeven sales is also provided. They are shown on a monthly (12 months = 1 year) and a weekly (1 month = 4 weeks) basis for comparison purposes. The required monthly and weekly Revenue to achieve envisioned goals is directly calculated from the top line of the Business Model. Then the annual Breakeven (BE) Sales are calculated (BE Sales = Revenue / (1 – COGS Factor)) and the monthly and weekly Breakeven Sales are calculated.

Based on these assumptions, the sample business model and 3-year projections are shown in the following table:

Business Model Analysis & Projections (Initial)

Financial Projections	Current	%	Year 1	%	Diff	Year 2	%	Diff	Year 3	%	Diff
Revenue	$100,000	100%	$120,000	100%	20%	$145,000	100%	21%	$175,000	100%	21%
Cost of Goods Sold											
Variable Expenses	$28,000	28%	$33,600	28%	20%	$40,600	28%	21%	$49,000	28%	21%
Gross Profit	$72,000	72%	$86,400	72%	20%	$104,400	72%	21%	$126,000	72%	21%
Fixed Expenses	$41,465	41%	$41,465	35%	0%	$41,465	29%	0%	$41,465	24%	0%
Operating Profit	$30,535	31%	$44,935	37%	47%	$62,935	43%	40%	$84,535	48%	34%

Breakeven Sales	Current	%	Year 1	%	Diff	Year 2	%	Diff	Year 3	%	Diff
Annual	$57,590	58%	$57,590	48%	0%	$57,590	40%	0%	$57,590	33%	0%
Monthly	$4,799		$4,799			$4,799			$4,799		
Weekly	$1,108		$1,108			$1,108			$1,108		

Sales Plan	Current	%	Year 1	%	Diff	Year 2	%	Diff	Year 3	%	Diff
Annual	$100,000		$120,000		20%	$145,000		21%	$175,000		21%
Monthly	$8,333		$10,000			$12,083			$14,583		
Weekly	$1,923		$2,308			$2,788			$3,365		

To optimize the business model, the 3 year projections are adjusted based on further qualitative and quantitative analysis. The first order of business is to determine the marketing and sales strategies that will be employed to achieve the envisioned 21% annual revenue growth rate. Start by using Porter's 5 Forces model (new entrants, substitution, suppliers, customers, competitors) to analyze the competitive environment. Then determine the proposed

Marketing Mix using the 7 P's of Marketing (products, pricing, positioning, promotion, placement, people, processes, and physical evidence).

Beyond that, additional analysis will be focused more on sales and marketing strategies to achieve your goals. Viewing this from a quantitative standpoint, you can look at your total number of customers, your number of repeat customers, your average order size, and the annual amount spent per customer, as well as the percentage of revenue your largest customer represents. It's also good to look at your sales conversion process in terms of the number of inquiries you have versus the number of prospects you have, to the actual number of customers that you have secured through the process. By analyzing this information, you can think about how to improve your results in these areas going forward. The strategy to increase revenues can consist of one or more of the following activities: increasing your pricing, selling more to your current customers, increasing frequency of customer sales, and/or selling to new customers.

Use this information and additional analysis to develop the best strategies for growing Revenue and achieving your envisioned goal. For example, you might be able to incorporate up-selling into the process, which can increase your average order size. You may also be able to reach your target market more effectively and improve upon your customer conversion rate. Obtaining customer feedback on your sales process, your product mix, your promotions, and PR may provide other ways to improve customer acquisition and retention rates. The four primary ways to increase Revenue are provided below.

Revenue Expansion Strategies

Increase Transaction Size	Attract More Customers
Raise Prices	More Frequent Transactions

It's also important to look at ways to decease Variable Expenses (COGS). Some common ways to do this are to lower your costs by purchasing larger quantities at discount, to seek new suppliers with better pricing, or to increase productivity in delivering your product or services to lower your variable cost percentage. In addition, you can become more productive with the labor. Reducing the Variable Factor is the most impactful way to decrease COGS and thereby increase Operating Profit. Additional strategies are shown in the image below.

Variable Cost Reduction Strategies

Volume Discounts

Shop Around

Increase Efficiency

Use Technology

Rework Product

In addition, it is important to minimize fixed costs without negatively impacting business operations or compromising product or service quality. One way many companies do that is through outsourcing functions such as payroll, accounting, or human resources. Other opportunities to reduce Fixed Expenses include negotiating reductions in your rent, greater use of technology/automation, and streamlining processes. Additional strategies are listed below.

Strategies to Lower Fixed Costs

- Reduce supply expenses
- Lower financial expenditures
- Modernize your marketing efforts
- Use efficient time strategies
- Harness virtual technology
- Narrow your focus
- Make the most of your space
- Maximize your employees' skills
- Focus on quality

Optimizing the business model to develop a plan for achieving your goals is an iterative process. It requires multiple updates and adjustments based on changes in strategy and assumptions. Each time it is important to compare results with the Operating Profit goals since they are more important than the Revenue goals.

Iron Strong Jewelry Analysis

Looking at Iron Strong Jewelry, Tina's greatest need is to increase revenue and profitability since the company already has a great name, differentiated products, and a passionate owner. The implementation of her marketing plans and sales strategies is the key to achieving her goals. Tina needed to be more creative and deliberate in her efforts to acquire new customers. Her tactics needed to be more active than passive, which would require her to expand beyond online and word of mouth advertising. She needed to transform herself, given her tendency to be introverted and hesitant to talk with new people. It was certainly possible, given how comfortably and passionately she communicated with people she knew. Tina's challenge was finding the right target market which we talked about in Chapter 2 where we used Iron Strong Jewelry as an example. From there we talked about the potential for expanding her marketing scope by considering ideas such as these…

- Partnerships – with gyms, Peloton (popular new at-home spinning concept), other trainers, nonprofits
- Cross Selling – jewelry and training, health and wellness companies
- Introducing New Products – t-shirts, exercise machines, videos, etc.
- Vending, Hosting or Sponsoring Events – bicycling, weightlifting, cycling, races, weight lifting, spa, fashion, etc.
- Narrowing target market to focus on a niche and then define the ideal customer
- Expand range of marketing and sales efforts to include networking, newsletter, e-mail marketing, trade shows
- Develop comfort level with and better content for communicating with people about her business
- Online – new website, social media, paid advertising, YouTube

We explored these and other marketing and sales opportunities to increase revenues for Iron Strong Jewelry. The goal is for Tina to "create a playground(s) where no one else is playing." This is what Michael Dermer calls thinking like an entrepreneur in his book *The Lonely Entrepreneur.*

Exothermic Analysis

Taking another look at Exothermic Molding from an analytical perspective, there were three key areas that stood out from the rest. On the positive side, they had the financial strength and flexibility to invest in further developing and growing the business, which many companies don't really have. This is very helpful for making improvements in the business, as well as paving the way for a succession plan.

However, on the negative side, Exothermic had staffing problems despite paying well and offering benefits. Most manufacturing companies in the State of New Jersey and across the country have significant difficulty hiring and retaining new employees, even as their current workforce is beginning to age out. It's difficult to find people who are willing to work in those conditions. To make the situation even worse, entry level employees start out sanding plastic parts to smooth the edges. This is not something many, if any, young people envision as their future career. In addition, a career path was not well communicated, so an employee's impression is that they could end up being a sander for a very long time. Furthermore, Exothermic has a need for cross-training so they have enough people skilled in different areas to reduce the potential for bottlenecks in their production process.

The next issue is part of the reason why they got so far behind. There was an opportunity to implement standard processes for managing production and increasing performance metrics. Exothermic did have an Enterprise Reporting System (ERP) but was not using it to its capacity. As a result, information about the business was not readily available. Plus, the information they had would need to be downloaded and analyzed to make it useful.

Recommendations

The purpose of analysis is to determine the most appropriate solutions to recommend. It involves determining the optimal way to go from where you are (Assessment) to where you want to be (Envisioning). In small business, there are always more activities than your resources can address. Prioritizing recommendations helps you to focus on the most valuable outcomes. To be successful, you should tackle no more than the three recommendations at a time (Top 3). Doing so avoids becoming overwhelmed and stagnant.

Iron Strong Jewelry Recommendations (Top 3)

1) Combine marketing and branding efforts for Iron Strong Fitness and Iron Strong Jewelry and expand range of marketing and sales efforts
2) Produce Fit Fest event during the holidays
3) Expand the Iron Strong product line to include t-shirts with edgy content
4) Read Dale Carnegie or take a course on it
5) Retool website
6) Update mission/vision to incorporate target customers

Exothermic Recommendations (Top 3)

Based on my analysis of Exothermic, there were three primary recommendations for things that needed to happen before Paul could even begin to work on succession planning and Key Performance Indicators (KPIs).

1) Organizational restructuring: creating more formalized structures, processes, procedures, and systems
2) Expand usage of ERP System and other resources to access key info on a timely basis
3) Work on personal growth strategies in preparation for a successful transition to becoming a manager of managers
4) Define A Career Path For Different Roles
5) Implement A Cross Training Program Including Time At Each Station

Learn more about topics discussed in this chapter from courses available at the Small Business Pro University (www.SBProU.com).

Key Learnings

1) Analysis helps you optimize the strategies used to achieve your goals
2) Always use the business model as part of your analysis
3) Focus on no more than three recommendations at one time

Chapter 11 – Step 3: Implementation & Tracking

Terry Trayvick is a world class business leader who turned around a billion dollar corporate business unit that was losing money. His leadership efforts resulted in profitability increasing by $80 million per year within a 3-year period. As featured guest speaker at the September 25, 2017 POWER BREAKFAST, he said that, "Strategy is necessary, but not sufficient," and talked about his six principles for successful execution.

1) Being clear on your aspiration
2) Creating the actual strategy
3) Ensuring you have the right structure to support it
4) Ensuring your culture was right
5) Aligning all your programs and initiatives to the strategy
6) Measuring everyone and everything

You can have the best strategy and plans in the world, but if you can't implement them, you're not going to be successful. As a result, successful implementation is the most critical step in "Running Your Small Business Like A Pro."

You will recall that we started our process by assessing the current situation, and then envisioned where you want to take your business. From there we performed an analysis, before making recommendations on the optimal strategies for achieving what you envisioned for the business. Next, we will develop an implementation strategy before executing the recommendations. Since tracking results is critical, we must develop actual performance versus the plan. Plus, tracking allows you to make important adjustments along the way to ensure optimal results.

Step 3:
SBPro® Implementation & Tracking

Operational Tactics

Performance Measurement

Implementation

Why not implement the recommendations immediately? When making changes in an organization, it's critical that your leadership and supervisors understand what's to be done and are 100% on board with the initiative. In addition, it is impossible to over communicate about the plan. By developing a rollout strategy, you will communicate much more effectively to your entire organization about where things are going.

Part of the implementation plan needs to indicate who is responsible for what part of the implementation process, so that there is accountability. Also, there needs to be measures of performance that can be used for tracking purposes. Once you're ready to go, leadership is onboard, and everybody knows their role and responsibilities, you can roll out the changes to your organization. During the rollout, it is important to begin your tracking and benchmarking immediately, so that you can see the impact of your implementation as early as possible - and maintain and track it regularly to ensure that things are going as planned. Anyone who has ever implemented anything knows that things rarely go exactly as planned - Murphy's Law. There is always some tweaking and adjustment necessary to achieve the desired results. By tracking closely, you'll see any deviations from your expectations and be able to adjust before ending up with negative results or take advantage of new benefit opportunities that you may have learned.

Iron Strong Jewelry

For example, while working with Tina Tang, there were three recommendations she implemented: number one involved combining marketing and branding efforts for the Iron Strong Fitness and Iron Strong jewelry businesses; number two involved producing a Fit Fest event during the holidays; and recommendation number three was expanding her product line to include t-shirts with edgy content.

Tina's implementation plan for combining her fitness and jewelry business lines for marketing purposes involved creating marketing collateral that communicated each of these business lines on different sides of the marketing card used as a handout with her company's information. It also included developing a weekly e-newsletter sent to her distribution list featuring fitness related content and highlighted both her fitness and her jewelry products and services. In addition, she planned to cross-market to her existing clients by making sure that her fitness clients also knew about her jewelry, and then making sure that her jewelry clients received information about her fitness programs, as well.

Tina conceived the idea of holding a "Fit Fest" event in early December to bring together fitness enthusiasts with fitness related vendors as an opportunity to build awareness, increase holiday sales, and make some extra money. She laid out the program, developed a marketing strategy, and created a budget to track its performance.

Since the price point of Tina's jewelry was around seventy dollars, she decided to develop some complementary Iron Strong branded products at a lower price point. This was expected to increase sales by reaching out to a wider number of people. The catchy slogans were designed to differentiate her further in the marketplace, and they also provide visible branding for her company. In addition, they are higher margin products than the jewelry which helps to increase her profitability.

Exothermic

Exothermic's organizational implementation strategy consisted of formalizing processes within the organization, as well as creating systems that provide useful information for managing the company more effectively. This boiled down to the following seven initiatives:

1. A structural plan
2. A staffing plan
3. A training program plan
4. The production process plan
5. An ERP integration plan
6. Metrics and reporting plans
7. Developing a planning process and budgeting plan

We focused on implementing the structural plan by delineating specific roles and responsibilities throughout the organization. From there, we worked on the staffing plan for their expected needs in three years and mapped how to get there from the current staffing levels. This includes creating a job description for each role in the company. While doing this, the leadership team started to gel in its production process planning. They were able to reduce the number of overdue orders by working together and meeting daily. They also created a more effective process for planning daily and weekly production schedules, along with tracking job progress. This resulted in a steady decrease in the order backlog from more effective manufacturing, as well as collaborating with clients on adjusting delivery dates.

With the production manager position not filled, all of the supervisors had to be involved in making things work. By doing that, they developed a more successful process to streamline production planning. They were then able to take this process and automate it by using their ERP system data and feed it into a workflow management system. After that, performance metrics and reporting could be done more effectively. From there a budget planning process will better prepare Paul to spend most of his time growing the business, as opposed to working within it. He will have better information to keep tabs on performance thus empowering his mangers to make decisions and to quote pricing more effectively. The leadership team will be able to utilize the real-time reporting and metrics to make better and timelier decisions. This helps to streamline their ordering process, organize production systems, and reduce the turnaround time on orders.

While implementing the new organizational structuring, I took Paul through the Value Builder Program process to prepare him for his new role. As a business owner, you must continually learn and develop to be able to take your business to the next level. As a result, Paul was able to better understand what was needed to achieve his vision, along with his role in the development process. The more he learned, the better prepared he was to position the company to create a sustainable business that can run successfully without him. More specifically, moving from being a manager within the business to becoming the leader of a management team that runs the business.

Tracking

Tracking the results of your implementation is an ongoing process. At the end of each year, the entire planning process needs to be reviewed and updated by using the three steps that we've laid out in the SBPro Methodology. Some people hear the word tracking and become fearful because they realize that they must use numbers and quantitative measures to do it right – refer back to what we learned in Chapter 3. There are also qualitative tracking measures that should be used based on the nature of your business. So, what do you need to track results and how do you do it? In many cases, it's as simple as laying out your expectations for results and then comparing actual performance to your plans to determine how successfully your recommendations have been implemented.

Sales & Marketing

If you're launching a new product, first and foremost, you want to track projected sales by breaking them down into daily, weekly, and/or monthly targets. You need to know the actual cost to manufacture and distribute your product(s) and/or service(s) in order to determine whether it is in line with your expectations. In addition, keeping track of demand helps ensure that you keep the appropriate amount of inventory and assess whether to increase or decrease prices. It is important to track the effectiveness of marketing campaigns relative to your expectations. Finally, you want to know how your competition responds to the new product and track how it is impacting the marketplace.

These are some of the measures you want to track because they are important to achieving the goal, and tracking gives you the ability to make changes throughout the year that will help to improve your company's performance rather than just waiting for the end of the year to see what happens. This allows you to be proactive, rather than reactive. Better information is required for you to make better business decisions, which is the key to becoming a successful business leader and being able to run your business like a pro.

Customer Service & Experience

You may want to obtain customer feedback on the new product to learn about opportunities for improvement - plus, it can help with determining your service quality and consistency. Surveys, live events, gathering information at the point of sale, mystery shopping, calling a sample of your customers, having a suggestion box, holding a contest, offering an incentive, monitoring online ratings, and the amount of returns are all methods you can use to assess how your customers perceive and interact with your business.

Financial Management

All businesses need to closely track revenue, the variable cost percentage, fixed costs, profitability and cash flow. Other important measures may include overtime, working capital, inventory, and capital expenditures for some businesses.

Iron Strong Jewelry

Now, let's look at the impact resulting from Tina Tang implementing her recommendations and how the actual performance is different from what she expected. In terms of combining her fitness and her jewelry businesses, she ended up getting a lot more fitness clients than she expected. However, the jewelry sales remained relatively unchanged. Many people knew her based on the jewelry business and didn't even realize she was a fitness trainer as well. One of her friends who was actually looking for a trainer noticed that she did training in one of Tina's newsletters and signed on to work with her, but never would have chosen to do that had it not been communicated.

We tracked the sources of Tina's online jewelry customers and found that pretty much all of them came through organic Google® searches rather than the paid online advertising she was doing. As a result, she was able to significantly decrease her marketing expenses. By learning who was actually purchasing her jewelry, she determined that it was mostly men buying gifts for a significant female in their lives to celebrate her fitness accomplishment. This revelation led her to target a different niche of potential customers that have the highest value for her jewelry products. Generally, they liked that Iron Strong jewelry was higher quality and could be further personalized through engraving. Many men had a lot of difficulty finding unique, personal gifts for their significant other and this jewelry fit the bill.

Tracking the progress of The Fit Festival event involved laying out the timeline of different milestones that need to be met. Tina tracked the number and dollars of vendors and the number of registrants versus her budget. She also looked at reaction to her online postings about the event. This allowed her to know where things stood on a regular basis to determine where and how she should spend her time and marketing efforts. In addition, she collected feedback and ideas from participants and vendors both through a survey and by chatting with them specifically about the event. One other thing that she tracked was the number of hours associated with planning the event. Based on the tracking, she was able to sell out her vendor spaces quickly and easily, while it proved to be more difficult to sell the individual attendee tickets. This led her to believe that her vendor prices were way lower than they could and should have been. She decided to raise them as part of the planning process in the coming year. She also ended up spending a lot more of her personal time producing the event than expected. Tina needed to become more efficient next year, now that she should be over the learning curve associated with her first event. She ended up selling a lot more jewelry than expected, which was great. It was also determined that she needed to start marketing and selling earlier in the year and that the attendees would have liked additional activities, such as a class or workshops during the event.

Based on what Tina learned and implemented at her Fit Festival, the next year she had a training class at the beginning of the event, which brought in more attendees; she had more vendors who paid twice as much as they paid the year before; and they sold at least twice as much as they sold the year before. That's a signal that she can probably go up on vendor pricing the following year. In addition, Tina made a lot more money and spent a lot less time putting the second Fit Festival together. Overall, the feedback from all parties was even more positive than the year before and both attendees and vendors would have liked to have another class or two available to them that day, which she plans to implement next year.

Tina decided to test the market for her t-shirt designs by trying out a single design in a limited quantity, using the methodology outlined in the book, *The Lean Startup* by Eric Ries. This allowed her to better gauge the market for this new product with minimal investment. She offered the new product while vending at a weightlifting competition event for women. Her experience was much better than expected. Having t-shirts increased the visibility of her vending table and enticed a lot of people to come over and see them, at the same time being exposed to her jewelry. Tina sold out of her entire inventory and took orders from people who weren't able to get a t-shirt that day. As a result, she chose to add a new t-shirt designs to be chosen from three options in an online competition she held after the event. Tina is now selling t-shirts through her weekly newsletters and continues to work on additional designs.

Exothermic

We developed a dashboard to track progress on milestones for each the seven initiatives outlined in Exothermic's organizational structuring plan. This provided a 1-page report, which is an easy way to update and to clearly see status on implementation of the recommendation.

<u>**Next Steps**</u>

The 3 step SBPro Methodology is an iterative process, meaning that it should be done again and again to continually improve your business. Each assessment will show how far you have come and the future you envision may change. Further analysis will produce new insights and will lead to better recommendations. Successfully implementing these recommendations and tracking progress will help you to achieve and even exceed your goals. This is how you do it!

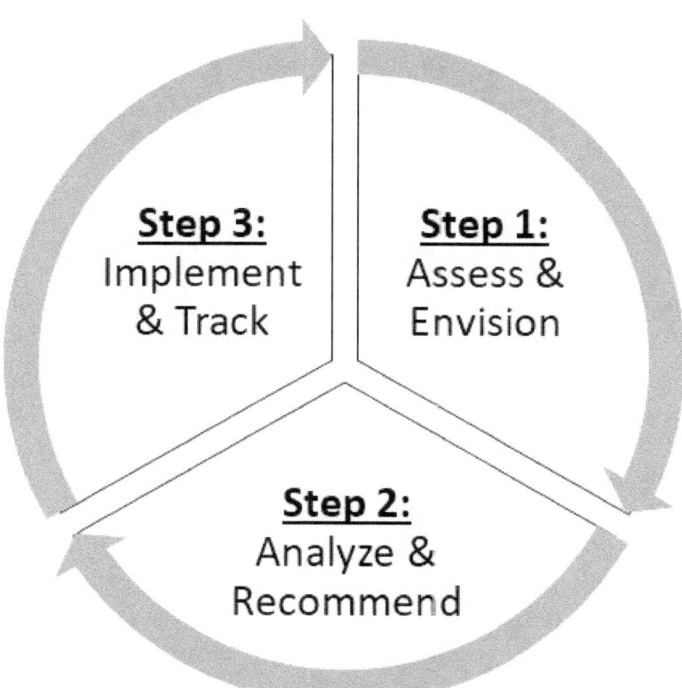

Learn more about topics discussed in this chapter from courses available at the Small Business Pro University (www.SBProU.com).

Key Learnings

1) Strategy is necessary, but not sufficient
2) Implementation plans require accountability
3) Track both quantitative and qualitative information
4) Compare performance to plans regularly and adjust as appropriate
5) SBPro Methodology is an iterative process

Conclusion

This is not the end - this is hopefully the beginning of a new upward trajectory for your business. I'm excited to have been a part of your growth plan and look forward to a continuing relationship ... and to hearing your own personal success story.

I appreciate you taking the time out of your busy schedule to learn about the Running Your Business Like A Pro methodology and hope that you have become significantly more knowledgeable about running your business more effectively. It was an honor to share with you my experience and those of our many clients and colleagues to better prepare you for some of the challenges and pitfalls you may face as a small business owner. Even if you only take away one thing from the entire book, it will still prove to have been an extremely valuable investment.

Going forward, the economy and competition will continue to become more challenging for small business owners, but the knowledge you've gained will prepare you to compete a lot more effectively against any size business - including Fortune 500 companies. Another challenge that you'll be facing is that more and more people will not be able to remain in the workforce as employees and will decide to start a small business to create income for themselves, especially those that are aging out, victims of corporate downsizing, or replacement by Artificial Intelligence and robots. But that scenario can also prove to be an opportunity because it will give you access to quality employees at a much lower cost.

Although this book covers a lot of material, and should have given you many insights, it only scratches the surface of what you need to know. That is why I created the Small Business Pro University (www.SBProU.com) with courses, templates, videos, tools, etc. specifically designed for small business owners. Also, *Leadership LIVE @ 8:05! – Talking Small Business* (www.LiveAt 805.com) is my weekly Livestream and Podcast featuring interviews with business leaders sharing their secrets to success. In addition, I am writing several books for expanding your knowledge on the topics covered in this book, such as:

- Running Your Small Business Like A Pro **Workbook**
- **How To Sell More With Customer-Centric Marketing;** Talk To Your Prospects, Not to Yourself
- **Market Your Business Like A Drug Dealer and Win More Customers**
- **Get Your Business Financed Faster and Easier;** The P.R.A.Y. System to Access Capital
- **Exit Your Business More Profitably;** The Keys to Effective Succession Planning

If you need immediate help, our Business Advisory Team can provide the customized support services that you need quickly, easily, and cost effectively. I can also be available speak or facilitate workshops for your organization either live or virtually. Learn more about the expert coaching, consulting, and training services we offer at www.SmallbusinesslikeaPro.com.

Key Learnings

Foreword

1) Anything is possible!
2) Your imagination is your best friend
3) Don't let fear of failure get in the way of actualizing your dreams and goals

Preface

1) Key to success is making good business decisions – the better the information the better the decision.
2) Two ways to gain knowledge in business: planning and preparation or losing money. Which do you prefer?
3) Learn from the bad decisions of others.

Introduction

1) Business environments are more competitive than ever for small businesses.
2) Most small businesses need help increasing their business knowledge, developing valuable relationships, and accessing important resources.
3) Running Your Small Business Like A Pro outlines a step-by-step process for guiding you to successfully achieving your goals.

Section I
What You Don't Know WILL Hurt You!

Chapter 1 – How Did I Get Here?

1) Be clear about why you are a small business owner and what benefits you seek.
2) Understand whether creating an enterprise is critical to achieving your goals.
3) Have and continually update a plan for growing your business knowledge, the capacity of your organization, and the markets you serve.
4) Follow the critical path of working IN your business (product and service delivery), then ON your business (business model optimization), and finally ON THE FUTURE of your business (market expansion).
5) Use the SBPro Methodology as your process for continual improvement.

Chapter 2 – What is My Most Import Job?

1) Know that your most important job is to market and sell, which should be done for at least 2 hours daily.
2) It is important to continually improve your skills by training, practicing, and learning from what other businesses do.
3) The smaller and more narrowly defined your target market, the more success you will have.
4) Branding is proactively working to create the image that you want others to have of your business.
5) People are not purchasing what you are selling, they are buying what they believe you're selling does for them. Focus on the customer and speak to their needs.

Chapter 3 – What is My Greatest Fear?

1) Doing the numbers is not as scary as it seems.
2) You can't understand your business if you don't understand the numbers.
3) Without numbers you end up working "IN" rather than "ON" your business.
4) The numbers help you to plan more effectively and anticipate problems.
5) Waiting will only cost you more money (i.e. good decisions vs. learning from bad decisions).

Chapter 4 – Where Will I Find the Money?

1) Your personal credit score and report are critical.
2) Having collateral is extremely helpful.
3) Your taxes must be filed and hopefully show that you are making money.
4) No surprises – full disclosure is a must. It's better to declare something negative than for it to become a surprise later in the process. Credibility is one of the pillars for being able to obtain financing.

Chapter 5 – Is It Me or Are My Employees Crazy?

1) Adding people inherently changes your organization whether for the good or for the bad.
2) Managing, hiring, and dealing with people is one of the most challenging responsibilities of most small business owners.
3) It is difficult, if not nearly impossible to be both a good supervisor and an effective manager at the same time.
4) Since you own the business, have control, and can make all the rules, only you have the tools to create a better situation.

5) Creating the structure, processes, and systems for a business is not necessarily easy or quick.

6) You must create an organizational structure before you can have processes, and you must have processes before you can develop systems.

Chapter 6 – Can I Get My Old Job Back?

1) In a business, you're taking a lot of personal risk; you're the last one to get paid - that is, if there's any money left.

2) As a business owner you will most likely be working harder than ever before and making less money than you expected.

3) It is not as easy as just up and quitting or giving notice because your business life is intertwined with your personal life both socially and financially.

4) Having a business is like raising a child. It will take center stage in your life and become part of your identity

Chapter 7 – How Will I Ever Retire?

1) An entrepreneur's job is to figure out how he or she is going to get out of his or her business.

2) As a business owner, you are 100% responsible for figuring out and implementing a retirement strategy.

3) Prepare for retirement early by purchasing permanent life insurance, paying Social Security taxes, setting up a retirement plan, obtaining disability insurance, and staying married.

4) Focus on maximizing the value of your business and developing a viable exit strategy or strategies. Start at least 5 years before you might want to sell.

5) Profits, not sales drive the value of your company. A range of 2 – 4 times profits plus assets minus liabilities provides a general indication of value.

6) Obtain a Value Builder Score to see how your company rates in each of the 8 key business drivers. Visit www.SBProValueBuilder.com.

Section II – This is How You Do It!

Chapter 8 – Running Your Business Like A Pro

1) Every business needs to have a defined process to move it forward.

2) Critical path for a successful entrepreneurial journey: working IN your business, then working ON your business, and finally working ON THE FUTURE of your business.

3) Most small business owners never even make it to working ON their business because they don't understand how or why.

4) You need to assess the current state of your business, analyze its needs for future growth, and develop and implement a growth plan using the SBPro Methodology.

5) SBPro Methodology concepts: Assessment and Envisioning, Analysis and Recommendations, Implementation and Tracking.

6) Give strong consideration to hiring outside consultants to help you through this process.

Chapter 9 – Step 1: Assessment & Envisioning

1) It is very difficult to assess yourself accurately - get help
2) The SBPro Assessment is a powerful tool that is easy to use.
3) Envisioning - you must see it before you can do it.

Chapter 10 – Step 2: Analysis & Recommendations

1) Analysis helps optimize strategies used to achieve your goals.
2) Always use the business model as part of your analysis.
3) Focus on no more than three recommendations at a time (Top 3).

Chapter 11 – Step 3: Implementation & Tracking

1) Strategy is necessary, but not sufficient
2) Implementation plans require accountability
3) Track both quantitative and qualitative information
4) Compare performance to plans regularly and adjust as appropriate
5) SBPro Methodology is an iterative process

Recommended Reading

5 Second Selling
by Paul Holland

10 Ways to Screw Up an Ad Campaign
by Barry H. Cohen

A Setback Is A Set-Up for A Comeback
by Willie Jolley

Blue Ocean Strategies
by W. Chan Kim and Renée Mauborgne

Built to Sell
by John Warrillow

DIVORCE: The Answers You Need Before, During & After
by Rosanne DeTorres

E-Myth Revisited & E-Myth Mastery
by Michael Gerber

Finish Big
by Bo Burlingham

How to win friends and Influence People
by Dale Carnegie

Lean Start-Up
by Eric Ries

Most Likely to Succeed: The Frazier Formula for Success
by Evan Frazier

My Business Plan Book
by Laurana Edwards

Spank the Bank: <u>THE</u> Guide to Alternative Business Financing
 by Karlene Sinclair-Robinson

Strategic Influence
by Dale Caldwell

The 1-Page Marketing Plan
by Allan Dib

The 7 Habits of Highly Successful People
by Steven R. Covey

The Lonely Entrepreneur
by Michael Dermer

The Millionaire Next Door
by Michael Dermer

The Richest Man in Babylon
by George S. Clason

The Wealthy Barber
by David Chilton

Think and Grow Rich: A Black Choice
by Dennis Kimbro

Who Moved My Cheese?
by Spencer Johnson

Why Should White Guys Have All the Fun?
by Reginald Lewis

Author Bio

Andrew Frazier, MBA, CFA, SBP

Mr. Frazier is the founder of Small Business Pro University and the Business Pro & CFO of Small Business Like A Pro, LLC. He is a **Trusted Advisor** helping entrepreneurs, business owners, and organizational leaders grow revenues, increase profitability, and obtain financing through a combination of coaching, consulting, and training services. As a seasoned business professional, he has a proven track record of delivering superior results for more than 30 years. Mr. Frazier's expertise in business strategy and financial management allows him to take a holistic approach to providing the optimal solutions for his clients based on their specific situation.

For nine years, Mr. Frazier has produced a quarterly POWER BREAKFAST event for entrepreneurs, business owners, and organizational leaders that focuses on learning business best practices, enjoying great networking, and gaining useful knowledge. These events have facilitated education, relationships, and access to resources leading to tens of millions of dollars of economic growth and financing for more than 1,000 participants.

Mr. Frazier served as Chief Operating Officer of The Executive Leadership Council. Prior to that, he was an Assistant Vice President at the New York Life Insurance Company. His roles included Investment Management (helped manage an $82 Billion Portfolio), Corporate Services (In-Charge of 1,000+ employees at the Westchester Campus), and Mergers & Acquisitions. He also served with distinction as a US Navy Supply Corps Officer on the USS Clark FFG-11 and was awarded a Navy Achievement Medal for outstanding leadership. He achieved the rank of Lieutenant Commander.

Mr. Frazier graduated from the Massachusetts Institute of Technology (MIT) with a BS in Mechanical Engineering and a concentration in Economics. He also earned an MBA in Finance and Management from New York University's Stern School of Business (NYU-Stern). In addition, Mr. Frazier achieved the Chartered Financial Analyst (CFA) professional designation.

Mr. Frazier is an active participant in numerous community and professional organizations. He serves as an advisory board member of the New Jersey Small Business Development Center – Rutgers Newark (NJSBDC @ Rutgers Newark) and is a Board Member for One Hawk Capital, LLC. He has also served in a leadership role and/or as a board member of CALIBR (formerly the NextGen Network), Urban Youth Action, Inc., The ELC Institute for Leadership & Development, and the Granville Academy. Mr. Frazier has taught workshops, seminars, and college courses on finance, accounting, and entrepreneurship.

Mr. Frazier has been married for more than twenty-five years, has two children, and lives in Montclair, New Jersey.

Websites

www.SmallBusinessLikeAPro.com

www.SBProU.com

Additional Websites
- **Livestream and Podcast** – www.LiveAt805.com
- **Blog -** https://www.sbprou.com/sbpro-blog

Social Media

LinkedIn
- Personal Profile: AndrewFrazier
  - https://www.linkedin.com/in/andrewfrazier/
- Company Page: small-business-pro-university
  - https://www.linkedin.com/company/71039316/admin/

Facebook
- Personal Profile: Andrew.Frazier.Jr
  - https://www.facebook.com/andrew.frazier.jr/
- Company Page: SBProU
  - https://www.facebook.com/SBProU/

Twitter
- @Andrew_Frazier
  - https://twitter.com/Andrew_Frazier
- @SmBizLikeAPro
  - https://twitter.com/SmBizLikeAPro

Instagram
- Small_Business_Like_A_Pro
  - https://www.instagram.com/andrew_frazier_sbpro/

YouTube
- Small Business Pro University
  - https://www.youtube.com/channel/UC1AMRZgquki0P8fRxoDk0KQ

Small Business Like A Pro

Helping entrepreneurs & small businesses owners to...

Grow Revenues
Increase Profitability
Obtain Financing

Providing entrepreneurs, business owners, and organizational leaders with access to the expertise, tools, and resources they need to compete effectively in this fast paced, technology driven, global business environment. Our services include:

- Coaching
- Consulting
- Training
- Speaking

155

Small Business Pro University (SBProU)

Mission

Helping Entrepreneurs and Businesses Owners Grow Revenues, Increase Profitability, and Obtain Financing.

Vision

Become the leader at providing entrepreneurs, small business owners, and organizational leaders with access to the expertise, tools, and resources they need to compete effectively in this fast-paced, technology-driven, global business environment.

Values

Using Creativity to effectively combine Knowledge with Experience for entrepreneurs and small business owners to achieve Continual Improvement throughout their journey to develop a sustainable enterprise.

SBProU Offerings

Courses
- Individual Courses
- Bundled Courses
- FREE Courses

Certification Programs
- Startup
- Small Business Pro
- Masterpreneur

Coaching Programs
- 1-on-1
- SBPro Strategic
- Masterpreneur Playbook

SBPro University Press
- Books and Workbooks

Membership Groups
- Small Business Pro Network
- The Masterpreneur Club

Leadership LIVE @ 8:05 – Talking Small Business
- Livestream – Tuesdays @ 8pm EST
- Podcast – Fridays @ 10am EST

Special Offer

50% Off

Selected Courses

https://www.sbprou.com/special-offer

Thank you for purchasing my book.

Andrew Frazier, MBA, CFA
Founder, Small Business Pro University
Andrew@MySBPro.com
www.SBProU.com

www.ingramcontent.com/pod-product-compliance
Lightning Source LLC
Chambersburg PA
CBHW071744120626
46550CB00002B/654